KEVIN COSTNER

By
TODD
KEITH

ikonprint
ikonprint/Publishers/United Kingdom

THE UNAUTHORIZED

BIOGRAPHY

First published in 1991
Copyright © 1991 by ikonprint
All rights reserved, ikonprint
Printed in United Kingdom
by Dramrite Printers Limited. Southwark London SE1.
ikonprint/Publishers

Library of Congress Cataloging in Publication Data

Keith, Todd, (9/29/61)

Filmography: p.
1. Costner, Kevin, 1955. 2.Actors-
United Kingdom-Biography. I. Kevin Costner/The Unauthorized
Biography
ISBN 1-870049-3-49
Library of Congress Catalog Card No. 91–77802

This book is dedicated to . . .

My
Mother

For her amazing capacity to have always been a friend
first, and a mother second. For all your love and support.

LIST OF ILLUSTRATIONS

PHOTO CREDITS

Greg Gorman/Gamma Liaison
Paramount Pictures
Globe Photos
Orion
Orion
Rex Features
Universal
Columbia

* A special acknowledgment to: Richard Corliss, Richard Schickle, Stanley Kauffmann, David Ansen and Pauline Kael for the use of excerpts from their film reviews.

This book is dedicated to . . .

My
Mother

For her amazing capacity to have always been a friend
first, and a mother second. For all your love and support.

LIST OF ILLUSTRATIONS

* A special acknowledgment to: Richard Corliss,
Richard Schickle, Stanley Kauffmann, David
Ansen and Pauline Kael for the use of excerpts
from their film reviews.

TABLE OF CONTENTS

There is no one with cherished memories of a favorite star or celebrity who wants those happy images destroyed.

The goal of this book is not to attack the image of Kevin Costner. He is a screen star whose first directing effort, *Dances With Wolves*, was nominated for 12 Academy Awards (it won seven, including Best Picture and Best Director for Costner.) Costner financed the film independently and had the satisfaction of seeing it gross more than $200 million.

His last film, *Robin Hood: Prince Of Thieves*, took the risk that audiences would flock to see the cherished Hollywood classic. They did, to the tune of more than $175 million. His upcoming *JFK* is directed and produced by Oliver Stone, who won the Academy Awards for Best Picture and Best Actor the year before Costner for *Platoon*. Shocking in its allegations about CIA/FBI involvement in the John F. Kennedy assassination, the picture should prove to generate a good deal of audience interest.

Therefore, one can safely assume Kevin Costner is a screen idol, a leading man for the modern age who is beloved by millions. For his ability to entertain millions with sensitive, quality films, I share this admiration. However, where I differ from those who admire Costner based on his career and press image alone, I must know all the information I can and assemble all the facts that can be found, good and bad, before being able to make up my mind about respecting an individual or not. It does no good to find out the "myth" you are admiring on the screen as the kindly father figure is in reality a child molester. One must be a good person as well as a good actor to be whole.

To this end, this book has tried to present the full story on Kevin Costner. Without Costner's help, this was impossible to do fully. However, the many quotes wherein reveal his feelings about many things, including: the Hollywood "system;" directing *Dances With Wolves* without studio support; his sex scenes with leading ladies; his "perfect" father, marriage and kids; his early sexploitation films; his production battles on the set of *Robin Hood: Prince Of Thieves*; and past failures as well as future hopes.

Suspicion is the only word that accurately describes my feelings about a superstar whose image is so red-apple polished that there are no mars. Kevin Costner, you will find, has flaws – but what man does not?

What is fascinating to discover is how that man handles himself in some of the most pressure-filled situations imaginable. Yet he is also a private man who has hopes and dreams, loves nature and enjoys complete carte blanche in Hollywood to direct, produce and star in his own films. Somehow the flaws that come to light make Costner human, but they do not tarnish the glow from his amazing accomplishments in a career spanning only 15 years at the point of publication.

There may be moments in this book where you find out that Kevin Costner, though he tries, is not always a "good guy." Yet you will also find out his amazing tenacity and determination in fighting his career battles against all odds in a town that hates to lose.

In order to paint this portrait of Kevin Costner, thousands of articles were utilized to assimilate "pieces of character" from Costner's experiences in his childhood, his high school days, his early career struggles, his film projects and with his family. Friends, working associates, film crews, Hollywood agents, directors, actors, writers, producers and even high school pals all reveal their feelings on everything from Costner's high school awkwardness over his small stature to his full-blown celebrity-hood. His wife's feelings on his sex symbol image are revealed as family members share their opinions on Costner and his life's experiences.

What finally emerges from all this is a picture of a man who loves his career and his family more than anything in the world. What also emerges is a portrait of a sometimes vain, childish, egomaniacal Hollywood power-broker who gets what he wants by refusing to settle for less.

All in all, the facts say that Kevin Costner is not very far removed from his screen characters: he is funny, intense, sensual, manipulative, sensitive, caring, selfish, and at turns a plodder, a loner and an exhibitionist. In short, he is simply complex. That is my assessment.

Now it is time for you to read the facts for yourself and discover if Kevin Costner, the man, is anything at all like Kevin Costner, the myth. Enjoy.

I would like to express my sincere appreciation and gratitude to Saul Mussry for his invaluable research assistance during this project. He was a treasure house of "film" information. My thanks also to *ikonprint* and Peter F. for the opportunity and the support.

PART

1

EARLY LIFE

CHAPTER

1

THE AWKWARD KEVIN

The life and early career of Kevin Costner does not read much differently than that of most people: sports, awkwardness with the opposite sex, father-son bonding, average academic performance, an inferiority complex and a middle-class background.

After school, Costner married his college sweetheart, took a marketing position and began having children. At this point, most people's lives travel a similar route, with all the joys and pains associated with life. However, this "average guy's" life was different. His name was Kevin Costner, and in Hollywood he is now closer to King than commoner.

Kevin Costner was born on January 18, 1955, in Compton, a lower-income Los Angeles suburb. His mother was a welfare worker and his father's job as a utilities executive meant the family had to frequently move around the state. Costner's roots are Irish and German.

Costner spent his grammar school years in such different communities as Santa Paula, Ventura, Visalia and Ojai as the Costners moved around scenic central California. By the time he was ready for Villa Park High School, he was enough of an athlete to letter in baseball and basketball and to play on the football team.

This nomadic existence was responsible for many of Costner's later insecurities. For instance, his penchant for proving himself by doing most of his own movie stunts stems from the days of proving himself as a triple-threat athlete.

The constant relocation was a necessary part of Bill Costner's duties with Southern California Edison, for which he serviced their electrical lines. Bill Costner was promoted to the position when Kevin was only six, and from that time on, the family began their frequent moves.

This sense of rootlessness made Costner feel he was unable to form close friendships, for as soon as he had, it was time to move on. It is also one reason he feels his academic performance was only average at best. Four high schools in almost as many years would tax even the brainiest student's ability to "keep up."

"I was always on the outside," Costner recalls. "I didn't feel 'there' until the end of the year, and then we'd move again." Still, sports was an outlet that could make him feel "accepted," and he threw himself into baseball and basketball, lettering in both while still being accomplished enough to play start regularly for the football team.

One interesting event occurred during a basketball game that, had anyone known who Kevin Costner would one day become, would have recognized as a forewarning.

The star recalls that particular game: "I had the exhibitionism knocked out of me. During one basketball game, I was knocked into the lap of a pretty girl. She was drinking a Coke, and I took a sip. There was a rousing cheer. Later my dad told me, 'You're out there to play.'" Even though his father was not keen on his "showmanship," however, he supported his son's sports activities.

"I think I like sports because of my father," the actor turned director/producer confesses. "He never insisted I play with him, which made it even more attractive. He's my ideal of how a father should direct his son," he added.

Sports played a major role sports in the young Costner's life, and the close relationship with his father was definitely echoed in the hit film *Field Of Dreams*.

"Sports, besides the obvious competitive aspect, is about sharing and being fair," he notes. "And I've always liked to roll in the dirt. When I was little, I wasn't 'it' very often in tag. You can translate that into acting. I don't get caught lying very often. I make sure that difficult scenes come off. I knew athletics made me happy, and that was due to being in the middle of things. I didn't have any examples to make me think a movie star is what I would become. I always admired movies and the people in them, but a film career didn't seem like a realistic choice for me."

Still, having to make new friends all over again every time he moved only added to his shyness and awkward feelings, making Costner in turn fantasize even more about the film heroes he wanted to emulate.

"I'd lose myself in the movies," he said. "I had a very active fantasy life. I can remember as a ten-year-old watching *How The West Was Won*, and certain moments made me tingle with the magic of it."

Speaking of how his father gave him "perfect" direction seems to differ from Bill Costner's impressions of raising his son.

"From day one, Kevin was his own person," the elder Costner recalled. "Once he decided to take charge of organizing a parade at his school. I figured it was too big a job for an eleven-year-old and said, 'Kevin, you can't do that.' And Kevin said, 'Dad, never tell me I'm not able to do something.' He went ahead and organized the parade."

"Never tell me I'm not able to do something" is a line Costner never forgot. Later in his career, when he was going against all Hollywood convention by doing things like making back-to-back baseball-themed movies and directing a three-hour Western with subtitles, Costner would have to repeat that line frequently to executives and other doubting Thomases. Like his father, he would come to prove them wrong, also.

As the star has warned those who like to impose upon his personal space, "I can be pushed about a hundred yards, but there's one inch that's really mine, and it's not a great idea for anybody to get in there. I'm kind of afraid of that ugly streak."

Daddy's boy was not always a joy to behold, however. In kindergarten and just five years old, Costner was always getting switched from the morning session to the afternoon session and then on to the principal's office. When he wasn't involved in fistfights, he was found throwing rocks at oil rigs as they passed the school.

One time, young Kevin made a terrific commotion by breaking away from the rest of the class and then leaping off the school roof, only to break his big toe. It was around this tender age that Costner remembers his first "cinema" experience.

"I believe in the magic of the movies, in the opportunity that something great will happen. I remember when I was four years old, in those pj's that have the feet in them, going with my mother to drop my brother off at the movies, and looking out the back window of the car at the big marque with the red letters in the rain, and my mother telling me they spelled 'Ben Hur.' And I never forgot that. But I never realistically thought I'd be in the movies. I thought those people were somehow mysteriously born on the screen," he remembered.

Another film experience that took Costner a while to forget was his nightmarish horror at seeing *Hush, Hush, Sweet Charlotte* at the age of nine. His terror over seeing the Bette Davis horror film was so intense that he started having nightmares and required a nightlight for some time thereafter. The experience made him even more insecure and a little indignant, he recalls.

As Costner grew, he became anxious over his 5' 2" height as a sophomore in high school. "I didn't get my growth until college," he says now. "My mother always told me I would grow. I'm 6'1" now, but I never got over being short. I never even dated," he remembers.

Those who view Costner as a sex symbol and a powerful Hollywood force would be shocked to learn he suffered from an inferiority complex throughout his childhood. Due to these feelings of insecurity, Costner became intent on seeking approval from those he cared about most. Approval from loved ones and those he cares about most is still essential to the actor/director/producer, even as he writes his own ticket in the film industry.

He explains his feelings from childhood. "I was a loner as a kid – small, gangly, with big feet, a real late bloomer – and I never even had dates. I was little, always the new kid on the block because we moved so damn much. I guess like every kid, what I most wanted was to please. I still do. As a kid, when my dad was coming home, my brother and I used to wait for him. He was a working guy, a lineman for Edison, and we used to race to undo the laces of his boots. My brother'd take the left boot, and I'd take the right, just really glad my dad was there. I wanted to please him so much." One imagines Bill Costner being very pleased with his younger son today.

In spite of his phenomenal success as an actor, director and producer, Costner says he had no inkling at that point in his life of his future vocation. Kevin felt film stars were dropped to earth by Divine decree from some lofty place above the heavens, not normal folk like he and his family. "I always figured that people on the screen were intended to be there. Acting was something other people did," he says. The Costners were close-knit, though, and Kevin's camping adventures with his father cemented their relationship on an intimate level that has remained intact to this day.

Aside from being close, the Costner family had always been nomadic, and true to his Hollywood perspective of things, Costner sees his father's life as something straight out of the *Grapes Of Wrath*. As he explains, "My father's side of the family lost everything during the Depression. They lost it all in the Dust Bowl and then came here from Oklahoma. They were Okies, like the people in *The Grapes Of Wrath*. They came from Guymon, Oklahoma in a Model A Ford, carrying with them only what they could fit in the car. What that gave us was a real common-sense approach to things. And there's this real need for financial security even now, when I've got more than I ever thought would."

This common-sense approach, coupled with the desire for financial stability, was a one-two punch for Costner when he tried to tell everyone in high school that he was interested in acting. Practicality won out and the future Hollywood titan was persuaded instead to enter college.

Costner was a poor student, but he had street smarts and played sports in spite of his small stature. In addition, he took piano lessons, wrote poetry and even sang in the First Baptist Choir. Yet his uneventful blue-collar existence offered the young boy with a great deal of imagination little inspiration.

Kevin was the third son for the Costners, his older brother Dan having been born in 1950. A second brother, Mark, died at birth in 1953. Kevin came along two years later and his mother was intent on instilling pride in her two sons.

"I remember our mother always saying to us, 'There's

nothing you two boys can't do,' his brother Dan recalls.

However influential his mother's guidance may have been, it is clear that the guiding force in Costner's life was his father. In a recent interview he said when asked how he wanted his own children to think of him, "like I think of my dad. My dad was a tremendous influence in on me, and I still talk to him every day. He's the kind of guy that if he borrowed somebody's lawn mower, when he gave it back, the tank was full of gas and the lawn mower was clean. He never missed anything I was ever part of, and I don't think I'll be able to be that for my children, given the way my job works. But I try."

The Kevin who was naughty in kindergarten was no better behaved in high school. During his junior year in high school, his brother Dan, who had served in Vietnam, was given a medal for heroism in the Marines. The Costners had to travel to San Francisco to see their son awarded his medal. In doing so, they left Kevin behind.

He didn't stay alone for long. Immediately, he invited ten friends to come over. In one of their nightly ruckuses, they broke Mrs. Costner's coffee table. No one had enough money to buy a new one, so they all stole over to a trailer park, broke into a mobile home, and traded coffee tables, making a mess in the mobile home so no one would notice the table when they arrived there.

That year was a difficult one for Costner, and he cut 73 classes that year alone.

Costner recalls his senior year in high school as being a very depressing and sad time for him. His beloved brother Dan was away in Vietnam and it made it "a very confusing time" for the high school athlete.

Furthermore, he missed three shots in one game, only to

realize he was beginning to experience vision difficulties. To this day, he cannot see without his glasses. Later, he experienced pain in his legs following a growth spurt. No one at this time, including Costner himself, realized he might one day be a Hollywood star.

"I didn't want to be an actor then, never even thought about it," he recalls. "But looking back, I think the signs were all there – the singing in the choir, the church musicians, the poetry, the creative writing classes – a constant urge to do that kind of thing."

His brother Dan recalls the constant relocation during their youth as a positive experience, saying it gave them "the ability to develop an inner confidence. You develop an ability to compete early."

Costner also had an urge to use a gun. His first, a big Winchester BB rifle, was given to him at the age of five. Like his character Jake in *Silverado*, Costner has always been comfortable with the feel of a gun in his hand. He was taught how to hunt at a very early age and he remembers the risks he took as a young boy who really didn't know any better:

"I remember private time as a kid, just sitting down with my gun," he recalled. "It's a wonder I'm still alive. I used to get into tunnels,. in irrigation ditches. I had no idea where I was gonna end up. I was real adventurous that way. My mother wouldn't see me until I came back and it was dark. The only requirement was, 'Don't go in your school clothes.'"

It is his love of guns and the outdoors that also made him fall in love with those nature-respecting, bandit-shootin' heroes whom he admired on screen. "I love what came before me," he states. "I admire Gregory Peck and Jimmy Stewart and Spencer Tracy. I want my kids to think of me as Spencer Tracy. From the time my brother and I were 7 or 8, we had guns, and Dad, he'd set the guns out, and away we'd go, up into the hills together, the three of us.

"He was my teacher and he taught me about loyalty, friendship and doing your best," Costner said of his father. "It's not a Boy Scout's creed. Truth and those things are never far out of style." Costner still tries to imbue the film roles he portrays with these heroic qualities of the old-timers he admires.

The pain Kevin was feeling over his brother's stay in Vietnam was used as an outlet to write. Dan would send him letters and diaries filled with his experiences overseas. Family, sports, conflict and movies were not the sum total of Costner's life at this time, although all were elements he would come back to use later. Costner was so moved by his brother's experiences he tried to write a book based on his tapes and notes. Like most people, he used the movies as an escape from a life he now found filled with loneliness, awkwardness and incapability. Movies may have been the teaching tool that gave Costner his eventual winning ways with the ladies, since in reality he was so shy and awkward around the opposite sex.

He very much recalls spending a great deal of time at the movies during these frustrating and sad times. "Great heroism, great love stories sent chills down my spine," he said. "I was particularly intrigued by dilemmas. To me, drama is dilemma – the fight *not* to do something. A dilemma is wanting to kiss a woman and not doing it. Once you do, it's action. Action is fine. I understand what it's about. But you have to understand where it comes from."

Being insecure and only 5'2," one hardly needs surmise where the kissing dilemma originated. After his steamy love scenes in *No Way Out* and *Bull Durham*, one can rest assured that kissing a girl is no longer a heroic dilemma for the sex-symbol actor.

Nonetheless, it was the dialogue and plots of these early films that instilled within the young loner a code of behavior – a sense of right and wrong. This code was built upon by his Baptist upbringing and small-town sense of decency.

Even though he may have mastered the art of the "kiss," Costner feels like he has always been an outsider and a bit of a loner. Even after he broke into films and became a major star, he still felt he was on the outside looking in.

He notes, "I've always been outside the movie industry; when I finally decided to become an actor, I didn't even know how one would begin. You live in an area called the Movie Capital of the World, but it was as foreign to me as it would be to you in England. It seemed like an impenetrable thing. I've hung on to all my old friends . . . I don't live in Beverly Hills; we have the same house that we bought ten years ago in La Canada . . . The house I would want to live in would cost $7 million and I don't have that kind of money. Honest."

Despite Costner's feelings of inadequacy all through high school, there were some girls who remember him as a stand out. Remembers Peggy Stevenson, a classmate of Costner at Villa Park High School: "I always thought Kevin was kinder and more sensitive than the other jocks. With his transition from athletics to film, those qualities shine through." Costner would pursue this change in a slow and roundabout way, but he sees this typical of the type of person he has always been. He likes the image of himself as a plodder, and feels the innocence can be an advantage at times.

For example, he relates a story about being a little out of

touch where the birds and the bees were concerned in comparison to his other junior high classmates. He retells the story: "I remember I was in the seventh or eighth grade. This guy was sitting next to me and he said he balled this girl, and I looked at him, and I said, 'Yeah, okay.' Then he says, 'I really balled her.' I was glad I didn't say anything, because two days later I figured out what 'balled' meant, and I never forgot that, because I realized how stupid I am about some things. I think I've always been a turtle, a plodder. I'm not surprised that what's happened to me has happened later, but now I'm where I always usually end up. The pattern of my life is that I've always laid back, and when I thought I understood what was going on, I would make my move."

Costner has always felt that, if such a thing as reincarnation exists, he was a pioneer in a previous life. He really feels like a kindred spirit with the Westerners who lived during the time when a man was a man, and justice was served by the barrel of a gun. After graduating high school, Costner built a canoe and traveled the same itinerary and rivers as Lewis and Clark did in their famous expedition to the Pacific.

When he was directing *Dances With Wolves*, Costner reflected on these feelings and the trip. "You know how Americans setting foot in another country sometimes feel totally at home? Well, for me, a country road has always felt right. The notion of a man on a horse, carrying all his possessions on his back, totally self-sufficient, is really romantic to me. When I was 18, I split L.A. and built a canoe, which I paddled down the rivers that Lewis and Clark navigated while they were making their way to the Pacific. So it's not surprising to me that I'm making a movie on this theme, about American and Americans. American history holds a real place for me."

After graduating Villa Park High School in 1973, Costner enrolled at California State University in Fullerton. He majored in marketing. "I graduated in 4½ years," he says. "None of my fraternity brothers did. They were all five and six year students. But I didn't know why I was going to school, the idea was to finish as fast as I could." It was early in 1978 when Costner decided to join the South Coast Actors Co-op. He appeared in various community theater productions, but he was not yet "courageous enough to make the shift." He continued on with his college courses even though his heart was not in them, and he really didn't know why he was in college – other than to please the traditionalists who ran the Costner household and paid his tuition fees.

What really made the college student know he had the desire to act was an advertisement he saw for *Rumpelstiltskin* auditions. He was sitting in an accounting class, bored, when he spied the announcement.

"It was the moment I decided to be an actor," he says. "I never looked back. I never breathed an easier breath. I relaxed. Then all I had to do was learn."

Costner recalls that when he saw the auditions for *Rumplestiltskin*, he realized he had a poor education where fairy tales were concerned because he wasn't sure if there was a prince in the plot. Assuming every fairy tale has a prince, he tried out for the play. From that point on, there would be no one who could ever dissuade Costner from following his true love again.

Learning his craft and traveling the road to fame and fortune would be a long and torturous one, but true to the lesson of the tortoise and the hare, Costner has surpassed many individuals who studied acting their whole lives.

It wasn't easy during this period either, though. There were the odd menial jobs, the financial worries and the need for financial assistance from his father, who frequently lectured his son. Costner remembers feeling wounded because he so badly wanted to please his father and have him think well of his choices. Bill Costner, on the other hand, was too conventional to think his son was making the right decision by throwing away the job for which he had spent years in college and earned a degree. His wife stood only a level above that where patience and understanding were concerned.

In spite of the difficulties, this period was a very eventful time for the future star because not only was he sharpening his acting skills and earning his degree, but he also met, fell in love with and married Cindy Silva, a Delta Chi at the college. It was March of 1975 that the fairy-tale relationship of Kevin and Cindy Costner commenced. As Cindy recalls about meeting her future husband, "it was kind of an awkward night for me because I was seeing another boy at the time and I went to [this] party with his sister. Then I saw Kevin. I kept glancing at him, but I had to be discreet. He asked me to dance and then he went away and then we danced again and he went away again. We danced five times. He was wearing penny loafers, his hair was slicked back, he had a sweater over his shoulders, and he looked so *sweet*. Pretty soon it was like Cinderella. It was about 10:30 and I left. I went home and woke up my mother." Little could Cindy have known at this point that the *sweet* boy in the penny loafers would one day be one of the world's most sought-after leading men.

Her Prince Charming also remembers the magic moment

when he met his bride-to-be. "I'd never dated very much, never did *recreational* dating, because Mother always said, 'It's very easy to fall in love, but never date a girl you wouldn't consider marrying.' Saturday night showed up and guys went into a panic if they didn't have a date. I never went through that. I just picked up girls. I was kind of used to sluts. I could talk to them. But when Cindy walked in . . . she was so beautiful, so *decent*, there was such a glow about her. She had these big, dear eyes." True to form, it would take the shy young man a while before he could get up the courage to overcome his chief dilemma at this point in life – kissing the girl with the "big, dear eyes."

Actually, the Cinderella story actually reads a little more like Snow White and the Seven Dwarfs. After meeting at the dance, they became a pair. During the summers Kevin would take off and go salmon fishing or help build houses and Cindy put on her Snow White costume and worked at Disneyland among the dwarfs and tourists. In the fall they would return to Cal State Fullerton and each other's arms. (In May of 1989, when the Disney-MGM Studios theme park opened and with an obvious soft spot in their hearts, they took part in the celebration.)

The couple married in 1978, when Kevin was 23. They both laugh when they think back to the fact that the screen's hottest hunk decided only after a month after their first meeting that Cindy cared for him.

After college, Kevin had his degree and a job offer. He took a job at a construction company, quitting after one month. His new bride came home one day after work to discover her husband home, sitting behind a table with pen and paper. He declared he had quit his job to act. He had zero Hollywood contacts and no agent, but lots and lots of

determination. Deliberately postponing the Hollywood game, Costner began gaining his acting experience and development anywhere he could. He admits that because of social and family pressures, he wondered if it wasn't too late at his age to follow his dream of acting. He notes, "It wasn't until the age of 22 that I decided to take up acting. I was on my way to a boring business career. I literally had to catch myself because I thought I was running a little late on the program. There's a notion that people know what they're supposed to do by the time they get out of college. And I bought into that system. But I started listening to my inner voice and said, 'You better do it, man.' The one voice says 'Grow up'; the other says to do the most ridiculous thing imaginable."

It is this pressure to know what you want in life at too early an age that can make individuals risk choosing something for their careers or lifestyles that will be a decision they regret for the rest of their lives, Costner believes. No such disappointment was in the making for the young man who had already told his cautious father at an early age, "Never tell me I'm not able to do something."

Costner soon became part of a group of actors and playwrights who shared the same dreams but he severed most of his connections with his "old world" lifestyle.

"I cut off all the lines and instead of working as a bartender, I worked as a stage manager at a movie studio – I felt that if I was going to take out trash, at least it would be *movie* trash," he laughs. "I also became part of a group of actors and playwrights." Costner believed that he needed to be around people who were not worried about piling up material gain at this point in his development.

Still, Costner suffered many frustrations as he and Cindy watched their friends succeed in their careers. When friends and family members asked him what he was doing now that he had graduated, he was often shocked to find their reactions registered from disbelief to downright rudeness. "Everyone thought I was crazy," he said, "to be throwing away everything I had worked for." Costner and his new bride had a hard time getting people to understand, so they became focused on their own lives and goals, while in the meantime Kevin kept on with his acting development.

His brother Dan remembers giving himself a five-year time limit to make his dreams of acting come true, but Costner now says he never had any kind of time line or deadline set on his making it. He was so content from having chosen what was in his heart and soul, that, on the contrary, he had never felt more peaceful inside.

Yet the reality was that he and Cindy had to support themselves while he not only tried to break into acting but for the first couple of years that he acquired the development and training necessary for a role.

For a final word on his early background and his own feelings about "making it," I turn to Costner himself:

"I'm *amazed* I got where I got. I don't know why the hell so much attention is paid to me or why so much money comes our way. There are a lot of good actors as good or better than I am. I'm glad it's happened, but I don't understand it. My background certainly doesn't explain it. Even as a small boy, though, I knew I loved movies – they made my face tingle. I wanted to be in those movies, and I don't know why that was. I thought those people were *born* actors. I didn't know I could ever be in them myself. I just liked to pretend I could. I really thought I'd end up just like my dad – a guy with a job and a paycheck, like most people. Nothing prepared me for this."

CHAPTER

2

EARLY CAREER

The real decision to become an actor for Kevin Costner, may have been inspired in some part by none other than Richard Burton. As Costner reveals: "On my honeymoon, just after graduation, I met Richard Burton on the plane coming back from Puerto Vallarta. I thought he was placed on that plane for me to talk to – but he had bought all the seats around him. I finally went up to him and said, 'I'd like to ask you for a bit of advice.' We got very personal very quickly. We talked basically about a hard life. I wanted to know if he thought it was possible to be essentially a good man and still be in this business. He said that he thought so, and that I should try. And he said, 'You have green eyes, don't you? I have green eyes.' The thing I liked about him was he never said it was a hard life, he never said the obvious." Costner would find out the obvious about being an actor personally through his next six years of sacrifice and struggle in order to become an actor. The "Face-on-the-cutting-room-floor" is the nickname Kevin Costner had during his years as a struggling actor. It was a name he worked damned hard to earn. In no less than five films, Costner had small or bit roles that were totally edited out of the films before making it to the screen.

As he came closer to the end of his college career, Costner was experiencing the urge to act. He joined the Southcoast Actor's Co-op where he studied and appeared in a couple of community theatre productions. "I didn't quite know if I had the courage. I'd always been taught that if you were going to do something, you had to put hours and hours into it... which, heaven knows, I hadn't done. But then I realized that my life was not written in stone at age 22," he remembered. Following graduation Costner worked little more than a month for a construction firm where he was supposedly involved in marketing. He recalls the inner-feelings that were stirring within: "I was confused. I didn't know what to do with my life. I knew I wasn't a suit man, a salesman 9 to 5. 'Jesus, give me direction!' By then I was married, getting odd jobs, trying to take acting classes. In class there were moments when I felt like a monster – that strong. I felt I was that good in that moment! That's when I knew what I wanted to be." Costner had to make a move because he felt he was just getting by on his looks and charm and wanted more due to his emptiness inside. "I said to myself, 'Boy, you're really skating by with just charm and American ingenuity.' There I was in marketing. A white rat could have been doing what I was doing. I prayed for direction. I needed essence. Making money was not the problem. Working was not the problem. What I didn't have was focus, a love of life."

The job at the construction company in a way was Costner still trying to please his father by taking a traditional route to success and stability in life. Yet, no matter how much Costner tried to do the "right" thing where his father was concerned, his inner desires and feelings won out. Yet, it is a sign of his great desire to gain his father's approval that he went to college before dedicating himself to acting. He also took the 9 to 5 job so, in his own words, "I wasn't throwing everything away that I'd worked for – because I didn't know if I was just running away from the world – I got a job with a construction company. It was called marketing, but that was just a fancy name for sales."

Unable to take the inner turmoil ignoring his heart's desire was causing him, Costner quit. Costner admitted this made him feel guilty. He was nervous about proclaiming to everyone that he wanted to "act" in the movies. His wife's reaction was typical, considering he'd given no warning signs of wanting to change career "horses" in mid-stream. "I quit after thirty days," he recalls. "Cindy said to me, 'What are you going to do now.' 'Act!', I said. 'What else?' she asked. 'I'm working on a screenplay. I'm a writer,' I said. 'A writer!' she screamed. 'You can't even spell!' She cleared the table, and papers flew up in the air like in a cartoon," he adds. Cindy's reaction shows that even loved ones find it difficult to support an individual who decides to tackle such a risky and major proposition as a career in film. Like Walt Disney's wife Lilly, who was terrified they would lose everything they had when Walt started fantasizing about an 'amusement park', Cindy was no less afraid and unsure. As Leonard Mosley reports in his *Disney's World*, "Lilly made her apprehensions [over Disneyland] clear to Walt in one of the sharpest quarrels of their marriage. She did not persuade him to change his mind but she did give him some sleepless nights and did make him realize that he could not afford to fail." With his brother Roy, the financial half of the business against the venture also, one shudders to think of a world in which the doubting-Disney's could have made Walt change his mind about building the "happiest place on earth." This lack of faith can be disappointing to someone with vision and imagination, someone who is trying to make the world a better and brighter place. Costner would do well to remember his own motto, that, when you are an artist you need to be around "dreamers." As an interesting aside, when the Costner's had three year old Kevin at Disneyland for the first time, he bumped smack into a gentleman's knees. When his parents discovered him, they saw that he had run smack into the legs of none other than Walt Disney himself.

Costner never forgot the feelings of doubt and uncertainty about his future at this often confusing age. At a UCLA speaking engagement in 1989, he would remind students, "It doesn't matter what you are doing now. You can change at 22 or you can change at 18, and it's really important for you to realize that you can do that. If you have a desire to do something, you just *have* to do that; you cannot settle for anything less than your own voice... When I decided to be an actor, I never looked back. Yet Costner can look back enough to realize there were few behind him in his courageous career choice: "Everybody in our circle thought I was going to be a hot-shot business man. Now here I was acting strange, talking about going to Hollywood to break into the movies." Instinct seems to be the one thing that has guided Kevin Costner when he has been unable to know for sure which direction he wished to take.

Jim Wilson, his co-producer later in his career (*Dances With Wolves*), is unaware how Costner could have survived as well as he did in a ruthless industry for which he had virtually little or no preparation: "I don't know where his instincts come from. His upbringing certainly wasn't in the field. He wasn't very well read. He didn't get good grades at school, but he has that whole streetwise thing and some life experience behind him that a lot of these kids in the business who are very pampered and went to the right academies and the prestigious colleges don't have. I don't think they have the same spine he had." Backbone and good instincts have been known to save many a hero in the short-term, but it is possible that, unless Costner backs up these qualities with some real book learning, he may become prey to mistakes over the long-term.

Costner does admit that he was worried and had some

fears during his early struggles as an actor, but, he did not let the fear stop him. "I guess I took a risk. But I felt it was a bigger risk not to do what my mind and heart were telling me. I didn't have a plan for success, but I never felt like turning back. Ever." Without an agent, Costner found himself standing in longer lines in Hollywood than he had during college admissions. Still, he was determined his day would come and he kept hustling while he waited. For the next six years he studied with private coaches, studying in actor's workshops and performing in a few student film projects.

For the first six months he went without any kind of work at all. He recalls these early days vividly. "I spent all my time auditioning, and looking for work in the industry – something that would keep me close to acting," he says. Finally, Costner found a position as stage manager at none other than Raleigh Studios in Hollywood. At Frances Ford Coppola's Zoetrope Studios he was listed as an extra. A casting director at Zoetrope from this period, Jane Jenkins, remembers Costner. "Somebody called and told me about this guy who was really nice and good-looking and said we should use him as an extra or something. So Kevin came over and he was a big, tall guy who was good- looking and smart. So we put him in *Frances*," she stated. Costner and *Frances* director, Graeme Clifford, were caustic towards one another and Costner's scenes ended up on the cutting room floor.

Frances was Costner's first bit role. The story behind the filming of Costner's "one-line" part shows all the signs of perfectionist behavior that he would later become infamous for. *Frances* was Costner's first speaking role and that meant, after six years of trying, he had won himself a role that had dialogue (i.e., he could get his membership in the Screen Actor's Guild). A lot of people told him, 'Just do a commercial,' but, he said, in reply, "It's not that *easy*." Nobody knew what he meant. The director of *Frances* and Hollywood were soon to discover what he did mean.

Frances was the nightmare story of actress Frances Farmer. The film helped many young actors win a speaking part and gain them a SAG card. Costner was supposed to play the role of actor Luther Adler. Finally, the time arrived for director Clifford to say the magic phrase, "Kevin, come up and say good night to Frances."

"No," Costner stated.

"Why not?" asked a startled director.

"He wouldn't do that."

"What," spluttered the director in total disbelief by now that this nobody young actor was analyzing his one-line reading as 'out-of-character.'

"Luther wouldn't do that. He's in this play with Frances every night. They come out of the stage door, he's going one way, she's going the other. He's got no reason to say good night."

The crew was irate at this point and a loud grumbling was overheard by Costner, who remembered it as sounding like everyone saying in unison, "Just say the fucking words!"

So, with lights ablaze and the camera rolling, Costner stepped out the door. Jessica Lange, playing Farmer, turned to him. And then he just walked off – without uttering a word.

"You've got to *say* something," the assistant director reminded him, trying to help his boss' growing migraine and hoping to save an inexperienced novice his Actors Guild membership.

On the next take, Lange changed her business. Instead of coming over, she waved. Costner thought that was really good. He felt the gesture needed no spoken response from him, so, measure-for-measure style acting, he merely waved in return.

This time the crew went bonkers.

When the fourth take was over there was a deafening silence on the set. The technicians decided Costner should be rigged with a body microphone, however, he spoke so softly on purpose that it was nearly inaudible. Yet, by four in the morning, the sound technicians had confirmed that Costner has uttered the line, "Good night, Frances."

One feels admiration for Costner in trying to make sure his only line came off "in character," however, one must scrutinize his lack of common sense in alienating a group of powerful professionals at this early stage in his career. He was not in the movie to act, he was in it to receive his SAG membership. In addition, he spoke the line anyway. Thus, one wonders if principles of characterization were really at the heart of the matter, why Costner didn't just refuse to speak the line flat out – SAG card be damned – instead of alienating the very people who were trying to help his career move further? Principle is principle. However, this example has not been included to support the idea that Costner should have acquiesced just to "get ahead." Rather, it is illustrated as an example of a work-related incident that shows why some of his colleagues and friends are beginning to show the strains of dealing with his "stay firm at *any* cost" attitude. Costner needs to discover that staying firm when you are hurting yourself (he almost missed acquiring his

SAG card, the whole reason he took the one-line role), and may be hurting others (the other professionals he offended and the extra costs from unnecessary retakes he created for producers on *Frances*), is not really staying firm at all – it is commonly referred to as "stubbornness."

On top of this, it is this type of stress that one can create for themselves unnecessarily that doesn't make life at the top in Hollywood any less problematic. For instance, when the scene was finally over in the wee hours of the morning, Costner recalls how he felt. "I walked to the bus – the extras' bus – and sat there, all by myself, and felt like a complete asshole," he admits with characteristic honesty. "I felt like crying. I said, 'What the fuck is wrong with you?' What was so fucking hard about saying that line?" However, at this low ebb the kindly assistant director came up to Costner and had a form for him to sign on his clipboard. Costner remembers he thought it was like receiving one of "Willy Wonka's golden tickets" for he knew it meant a SAG card.

Ironically, the scene was cut out of the film after all this trouble. Also ironic, and unbeknownst to Costner, this was the first, in a long series of roles, that would end up on the cutting room floor. So many would his "cut" scenes number over the next five years, that he became known as the "Face-on-the-Cutting-Room Floor." In his defense, the actor has said, now that he has become a big enough star to speak whichever and how many lines he chooses, "Henry Fonda wouldn't have said anything, and Paul Newman wouldn't have. Because it didn't mean anything. It wasn't right."

During this period in his career, Costner became known for the films he wasn't in more than for the ones he was. He had a bit part in "Stacy's Knights," a small non-union picture. The film was not a success, but what was interesting about its production is that the screenwriter was Michael Blake (who would later go on to win the Oscar for Best Screenplay for *Dances With Wolves*). Costner secured the role all on his own. It is a movie with a gambling theme, and, Costner's character is thrown over a bridge and drowned. He also had a bit part in the 1984 murder mystery, *Shadows Run Black*. He played the main suspect in this, his second shoe-string budget picture. More film opportunities started to come his way at this point, however, he was cut from most of them before they reached the screen.

Other than the role in *Frances*, Costner also almost made it to the screen in bit roles that eventually got totally cut from *One From The Heart*, *Table For Five* and, most famously, as Alex, the man who's dead in *The Big Chill*. *One From The Heart* was a Coppola directed film and *Table For Five* was a Jon Voight starring vehicle. Costner was cut from both, but not before adding more experience to his resume, if not actual screen appearances. Costner did get one line in the 1982 box-office success, *Night Shift*. There is a scene in the movie during which fraternity boys try to raid a morgue. The first frat boy that busts through the door is Costner.

In Lawrence Kasdan's *The Big Chill* Costner was selected to play Alex, the man who's already dead when the film opens. Costner's big scene was in a ten minute flashback which shows Alex's character. Ten days before the film hit the screen, Costner was called and informed by Kasdan that the role had been cut. As Costner recalled it, "He said, 'How're you doing Kevin?' And before he spoke another word, I said, 'You cut me out of the film, didn't you?' To say I wasn't mildly disappointed would not even be human, but during the making of the movie, I was very comfortable with being an actor and rehearsing and understanding what the work is all about – and what occurred there is what led up to today." Two years after *The Big Chill* had been released, Costner was able to admit the real reasons his character had been cut from the film, and the fault was not *his* he assures. "The character had to be cut," he states, "he was so unlikable as written and in the flashback scenes I shot that you wonder why all these people would get together and mourn him." One person who saw the screening of the film with the "Alex" flashback scenes in tact said, "If they'd kept him in, it would have sunk the film."

Tenacity and drive are what Costner is all about and these early disappointments did not prevent him from continuing with his goals. "I never thought about doing anything else," he says. "Time-frames and calendars are not good for this business. I think it's important for anybody who makes a decision to be an actor to never refer to themselves as anything else." After these editing room fiascoes, Costner got a film role assignment in Greece, but by the time he flew there, he was told his character had been eliminated from the script. Undeterred he came back to Los Angeles and found representation at the William Morris Agency. They set him up for a role in the upcoming John Badham directed, *WarGames*.

At this time, though, Costner was approached by Lawrence Kasdan who was assembling his cast for *The Big Chill*. Kasdan offered him the role of Alex, the suicide. The character was supposed to be seen in a series of flashbacks, but as mentioned, this did not occur once filming was complete. However, Costner chose to drop out of *WarGames* due to his belief that Alex was a good career move. The powers-that-be decided Alex should remain only a memory, and Costner was immediately flung back to a low-point where his career was concerned. "I didn't rely on sending resumes or 8-by-10 glossies," he recalls. "In fact, I'd walk out of their offices with my fingers in my ears so I wouldn't have to hear someone who didn't know as much as I did telling me what to do."

It was a series of just these types of meetings that made Costner learn to handle the rejection that comes along with the territory when one chooses to be an actor. As any actor will confess, though, self-doubt from disappointment and rejection can erode the strongest self-confidence and commitment. The series of editing fiascoes that gave Costner a better reputation for being "cut out" of films than "acting in" them could momentarily leave him pondering his choices. "There was a feeling after I was cut out that it would all pass me by. But I had confidence that my career wasn't dependent on *The Big Chill*. And I knew what a real American hero would feel: Look, I'm not in the movie, I don't want to get mileage out of that. Two years from now, if I emerge, it will be an interesting story."

Kasdan, who also wrote *Raiders Of The Lost Ark*, expresses his initial impressions of Kevin Costner: "He had never had a major part in a movie and suddenly he's in a room with Kevin Kline and Bill Hurt. When the time came and I had to tell him he wasn't in the movie, he reacted amazingly well. I think he was unhappy, but the experience was so valuable to him that it didn't destroy him. I said, 'It hurts me as much as it hurts you.' And I said we'd do something else, which turned out to be *Silverado*. I think I actually wrote it for him."

The star recalls a time during these struggling years when he met with a potential agent: "He was such a dick. He said to me, 'Look, Donald Pleasence will make more money for me this year than you will ever make in the business.' I was looking around, wondering if I should just crush his larynx right then and there." During those tough times Costner took odd jobs in construction and worked as a fashion print model. All of his fashion shots showed him looking strong and stiff. He was a little uncomfortable with the image and remembers the photos, "didn't even look like me. They kept sticking all this crap in my hair." Costner was supposed to appear on the cover of the January 1982 GQ (photographed by Barry McKinley). He was paid a whole $75 for his time and then, true to his early film career, he was bumped from the cover by Zubin Mehta.

In exchange for his acting lessons at Richard Brander's Studio City workshop, Costner did some construction for Brander. Brander remembers Costner's desire to succeed was "obsessive." He also recalled that, "Kevin's dedication was far superior to anyone I've ever had in class. There was a compulsion to learn and an acute self-awareness." Yet, Brander suggests that the struggles the unknown actor had with the obsessive desire he had to endure left him with some permanent scar tissue. "If you look closely at his eyes the door is shut. I'm sure there's some scar tissue. There's gotta be."

Nonetheless, Costner remembers *The Big Chill* as a turning point for him emotionally and career-wise. He learned his instincts about acting had been right while observing Kasdan and his select cast of talented actors in *The Big Chill*. "I had been wandering, wandering, wandering. Acting had always been holy to me, and finally I found people who felt as I did. It didn't break my heart to get cut out. I could get cut out of a million movies, but getting cut out of a $100 million hit, that was *something*." Later on in his career, Costner would lament that there were more moments cut out of his starring roles that remained on-screen than all the minutes cut-out of films from the roles he lost during his development years: "Hell, I had more moments cut out of *The Untouchables* and *No Way Out* than were ever cut out of *The Big Chill* and all my other films back then. That's the reality of film. Somebody believes it has to be speeded along. Or that the audience gets restless. And I don't feel that. I think people get restless if they don't enjoy the characters or if the story doesn't hang together. And there's the argument. Can you, by going *longer*, hold the story more." Costner would do just this in his longer-than-thought-commercial three hour production of *Dances With Wolves*.

That kind of control would take the next decade for Costner to earn. Yet, due to *The Big Chill*, word got out that there was a new kid in town. Michael Blake recalls his first impressions of Costner at this time: "He looked like a kid who'd just finished basketball practice. But even then producers and casting directors saw the footage and said, 'Hey, this guy could be a leading man.' Everybody knew. After that picture he got an acting agent. Before that he'd been represented by a modeling agent." Costner can be so charming that even his ex-agent from this period has only positive things to say about him. J.J. Harris handled Costner's early career. He says about his now very famous ex-client, "he's going to live a long life without ulcers. I think he'll have a multidimensional career unlike anybody else's. He has such a huge appetite for life. He's never satiated, but always satisfied and happy. It's true of all great people. He cannot get enough of it."

The experiences he faced during this struggle period were not easy for Costner. He and his wife Cindy attended parties where all their friends they had graduated college with were talking about their "new home," or career success. All Costner could talk about was an upcoming audition that he might not even get. In order to help pay the bills, Cindy took a job for an airline company to help with the rough times. It was one of the most frustrating and painful periods of his life, the actor admitted. "Cindy and I used to get together with friends who were all getting promotions and buying their second houses. We'd have these long drives home at the end of the night, and I'd say, 'What am I doing? I don't have a BMW. I don't have a lawn with dichondra.' But I called myself an actor, and I knew that someday this would all happen," he recalled. The actor's faith was helped by the faith his wife had in him as well, but he still admits of his struggling-actor years, "It was a school of hard knocks, but I watched and learned and the rest is history."

A part of Costner "history" many individuals remain unaware of is the fact that he's done a few sexploitation films currently available on video. *Sizzle Beach*, *U.S.A.*, *Gunrunner* and *Chasing Dreams*. Once he started getting known, cheesy Costner product began flooding the video marketplace. *Chasing Dreams* is available from Prism Entertainment, *Gunrunner* is on New World and *Sizzle Beach* is from Troma/Vidmark. The videocassettes are the attempts of those who made the films to cash in on Costner's unexpected success. Costner has no ancillary rights to the videos so he is unable to gain anything from their video release except for maybe embarrassment. Costner has legal precedings pending against the makers of *Chasing Dreams*. Due to the success of *Bull Durham* and *Field Of Dreams*, Prism Entertainment packaged the video with Costner on the cover in a baseball uniform (even though he is not seen playing baseball in the film).

Sizzle Beach, USA was originally titled, *Malibu Hot Summer*. It was made in 1979 and was actually Costner's first role. A low-budget T & A picture, *Sizzle Beach*, was being directed by Richard Brander – who happened to be located at Raleigh studios where Costner worked. Costner asked Brander for an audition and found he won the role of second male lead. He played a wealthy cowboy who falls in love with a well-endowed young lady. The lady was none other than the director's wife, Leslie Brander. This not only counts as Costner's first flick for fans who are counting, but it also contains his first on-screen love scene.

Eric Louzil, producer of *Sizzle Beach, USA*, and now a low-budget director, recalls: "We always laugh about that scene. He had to make love to the director's wife in front of a fireplace. He was real nervous and stiff. He kissed her, but it was like he wasn't into it." Costner was paid nothing for his first "acting" job. Louzil was also the producer of *Shadows Run Black*. When his career began to take off, Costner became worried about these sexploitation flicks. As Louzil tells it: "Kevin called me and inquired about the possibility of buying the films so as to shelve them." Costner never did acquire the rights and *Sizzle Beach, USA* was released on video in 1989. Regardless of its sleazy nature, Costner admits it still represented his beloved "acting." It was shot on weekends with my acting teacher as director. My scenes were with his wife so I had absolutely zero conception of what was really going on. But the experience helped me. I suddenly knew what type of actor I really wanted to be – and acting became holy to me," he says making no apologies. However, he does warn other young actors that he made these films as part of the, "Just do anything, make anything," syndrome.

When Costner really gets going on the subject of his sexploitation films, he sounds like an 1860s Marshall wanting justice: "The idea of working was very important to me ten years ago. I can't say that I don't have a flawed career. You can see I did. The fact that people capitalize on something like that seems to be a function of modern society. That couldn't happen a hundred and fifty years ago. Those people would have had to answer to me personally in terms of real justice and not something that's litigated." At least it taught him what he didn't want to do. Together, these sexploitation films amount to very little in the career of Kevin Costner. However, it should express to others how difficult it is to break into a field as competitive as acting, that, even someone who scales the heights of the profession – as Costner has come to do – must pay their dues at some point.

As he was beginning to doubt he should ever have left his marketing job, Costner was hired for the PBS production of "Testament." It was a small role, but the audition for the role was indicative of the future for Costner. Margery Simkin was the casting director. She has vivid memories of the day she met Kevin Costner: "I was auditioning people in a big office building where there were a lot of secretaries. And Kevin was just sitting in the waiting room wearing jeans and looking like he hadn't shaved – he just looked like a schlump. But after he left, every woman in that waiting area, and every secretary came in and said, 'Who was that guy?!' I've never seen anything quite like it; they just went crazy over him. It's probably the only time I can think of where that happened. I was never surprised that he became a star." After *Testament* Costner's career would take off with three films starring him produced in 1985 *Fandango, American Flyers,* and *Silverado.* For his co-starring role in the nuclear holocaust themed production, he earned positive reviews and quickly won the lead role of Gardner Barnes in *Fandango.*

When he read the script for *Fandango* and found out that he was in almost every scene, Costner's reaction showed his flair for humor. "They're going to have to stay up nights thinking how to cut me out of this one," he commented. He also said, "Gardner is charming, magnetic and manipulative. Best of all, he's in the movie." *Fandango* was an Amblin Entertainment production (Spielberg's production company) written and directed by the then unknown Kevin Reynolds. Frank Marshall and Kathleen Kennedy were executive producers and Costner had co-star support in the form of Judd Nelson, Sam Robards and Brian Cesak. No one could have possibly known at this point that Reynolds and Costner would become the formidable team behind *Robin Hood: Prince Of Thieves.*

Costner also did an *Amazing Stories* episode for Steven Spielberg, called "The Mission." Spielberg liked working with him so much he sent him a bomber jacket Costner wears to this day. Aside from these little known film roles and edited bit parts, Costner has also turned down many films roles that would make a less-in-demand actor cringe. He turned down *Platoon* without even meeting with Oliver Stone. He did this because his brother was a Vietnam veteran who was damned proud of the fact that he came back and set up a decent life for himself and his family. Costner, turned the role down flat out of family loyalty, but says now that, he may have been misreading the message of the film: "I had a chance to be in *Platoon.* I think that's maybe one of the mistakes I made. My brother was a marine in Vietnam, and he's had such a problem with Vietnam movies that have shown vets as wigged-out guys. He's very proud that he came back and made a life for himself, that he went to college and has a family. And when I read *Platoon*, the murder theme just jumped out at me so much that I thought, I can't do this to him. But maybe, in retrospect, I should have tried to be in the movie. In fact, *Platoon* was real and it was right. It ended up being about more than just murder."

Costner also turned down a chance to play the Willem Dafoe role opposite Gene Hackman, his *No Way Out* co-star, in the hit film, *Mississippi Burning*. Other roles that the actor has turned down over the course of his career include; the lead in the Costa-Gavras film *Betrayed*, the Alec Baldwin role in *The Hunt For Red October*, the Taylor Hackford directed *Everybody's All American*, and, as already mentioned, Badham's *WarGames*. Costner turned down the chance to work with Hackman and Connery because he felt the roles would be perceived too closely to the type of relationship he had with Hackman and Connery in *No Way Out*, and *The Untouchables* respectively. He didn't want to be involved with *Betrayed* because he got interested at the same time in Phil Alden Robinson's *Field Of Dreams*. He went against the advice of everyone he knew to turn down the Costa-Gavras film to do his second baseball movie in a row. Costner also had the good sense to turn down the films *The Ice Pirates*, *Grandview, USA*, and the infamous *Shanghai Surprise*. He's also tried to land a few roles that remained out of his grasp – most notably the roles in *Mask* and *The Killing Fields*.

Another role that Costner wanted but did not get was the lead in the 1981 picture *Mike's Murder* which would have seen his vulnerable "aw-shucks" heroism pitted against the down-to-earth intensity of Debra Winger. Casting agent Wally Nicita recalls the time Costner came to read for the part, along with some 200 other nameless hunks. Though he didn't get the role, Nicita knew enough to know she was looking at "star material. "Without batting an eye Kevin gave an absolute perfect, incredible cold reading – and he was gorgeous. The kid just had it when he walked into that room. He has all the natural instincts of the greats," she said. Nicita was the casting agent who recommended Costner go to Lawrence Kasdan, who was casting *The Big Chill.* She also recalls the noble reaction this youngster had when he found out his scenes were cut from the Kasdan hit: "He took it far more sanguinely than I would have. That shoot matured and nurtured him. It thrust him into a professional attitude. He came out feeling there was far more to this acting thing than meets the eye. It galvanized him and led him to prove he had the acting chops, to himself and to them."

Lawrence Kasdan felt he owed something to the young actor he cut out of *The Big Chill.* He wanted to do something for Costner since he had lost the role in Badham's *WarGames* solely to take his part in the Kasdan picture. Kasdan admits that Costner knew the role was not his for the taking, he had to earn it. He did and *Silverado* would be the film that allowed Costner to never look back. Kasdan had nothing but good feelings towards Costner, and perhaps still a little professional guilt over the big chill he gave to Costner's screen footage: "Kevin is a smart actor who makes good choices – a classic American star who is also a good actor. He was never desperate. Kevin's a contributive actor, clean and straight to the point. I wrote Jake in *Silverado* for him; I felt I owed him one after *Chill.* But he knew it wasn't his just to take – he won it. Then he had a million ideas for Jake. He came up with great stuff. He's very inventive. He thinks about his character in the best way – not as self-aggrandizement or scene-stealing – but about what else this character could be doing. What he can do is unlimited." During this time, John Badham immediately hired him for his upcoming film *American Flyers*, and Steven Spielberg (a Kevin Reynolds supporter and mentor) was instrumental in helping Costner get his role in the film *Fandango*.

CHAPTER

3

FANDANGO, AMERICAN FLYERS & SILVERADO

Fandango is the story of five close friends whose crazy days of college camaraderie are coming to an end. As a result, Gardner Barnes (wearing a pair of busted shades and the $18 tuxedo he purchased for a cancelled wedding) suggests they take one last epic adventure together – *before* they become "innocent critters squashed on the highway of life." Costner admitted his fraternity brothers were similar to *Fandango's* crazy crew, but he was always too busy to be involved with them. He and director Reynolds enjoyed the experience immensely and they found they had more in common than most people. As Reynolds puts it: "We have similar backgrounds. I was an air-force brat. You tend to live inside yourself. You create your own fantasy world. You develop an active imagination. Maybe that's why he does what he does and I do what I do. What you learn is not to get close to people."

Reynolds recalled the day a tall good-looking little-known actor named Kevin Costner walked into auditions: "We had already auditioned over 200 people for the role of Gardner Barnes. Just as I was getting frustrated, in walked Kevin. Within 15 seconds after he started reading the lines, I knew he was the guy." The movie was not a hit by anyone's standards, failing to gross more than $2 million in the US and Canadian markets combined. To this day, Costner remembers the film and the role fondly. Costner was able to work with Sam Robards on this production, the son of Lauren Bacall and Jason Robards. Chuck Bush is a 365-pound Belushi type slob who has a role in the film. Costner and Reynolds came across him in the "7- Eleven." The film was often unfunny and the action redundant. Still, Costner feels a part of Gardner Barnes is closer to him than most people might think.

Nothing great is achieved without enthusiasm, reminds Emerson, and enthusiasm certainly described the young Costner trying to break into acting. He describes his first audition: "I was screaming down a Los Angeles freeway, I was late and the car died. I left it right on the freeway, hopped a fence and hitchhiked to the audition. I mean I was on fire to get this thing." Costner stars as Gardner and, once the adventures take off, the boys sow wild oats, steal cars, hunt for treasure and, most importantly, bond with each other through the experiences. Reynolds direction is at its best when the boys are on the road, but the rest of the time it lags.

American Flyers was a John Badham film. After dropping out of Badham's *WarGames* due to his desire to work with Kasdan in *The Big Chill*, Badham was impressed enough to still want Costner for a role quite different than any he has played before or since. In *American Flyers* Costner was hired to play a low-key straight-laced doctor (who just so happens to be a competitive cyclist). Costner did all his own pedaling for the film, another example of how his athletic prowess allows him to add dimensions to his characters, that a less physically able actor might not be able to give. He plays Marcus, a man who doesn't say a whole lot even when he's talking. There's nothing on the surface to interest us. He's the type of guy that if there were not something burning inside, he would put you to sleep. That burning something inside was more than amply supplied by Costner's intensity. As Kasdan comments about the energetic star: "Kevin is voracious. He takes a part and wrings it out and eats it up. He just makes everything out of it that he can. He's incredibly inventive and full of this wonderful energy." At that point in time, Kasdan also noted, "I think he's going to be a big star," a prediction that would have made Nostradamus proud.

One of the co-stars Costner worked with in *American Flyers* was Rae Dawn Chong. Chong was just beginning to try and make a name for herself. She had no idea Costner would be a major star, but she does remember feeling that he was incredibly sexy and a "real" man. Chong plays the character of Sarah, Marcus's strong-willed live-in girlfriend and the ex-wife of a past racing rival. As she puts it, "Kevin is sexy and very mysterious. He's not girly at all, like some men who know they're attractive. He's a real man. He's like Robert Redford or Clint Eastwood – tough in the real sense." Critics have also compared Costner to Redford in the shrewd way he packages his image and gains control on his projects. He also would become quite similar to Clint Eastwood by directing and producing his starring role in *Dances With Wolves*. However, these types of comparisons would not be Costner's just yet. He would still need to earn that kind of Hollywood clout by becoming one of the most successful box-office attractions in town. Yet, the producer of one of his future films, Laura Ziskin, producer of *No Way Out*, knew Costner possessed similarities to these types of leading men. She noted, "I had my eye on him for a long time when I had hired him as the leading man (even before hiring the director), because there was a time when there was Redford, McQueen and Eastwood, but now there's only Harrison Ford and Kevin Costner... and Ford, at 44, isn't always what you are looking for" as a leading man.

American Flyers is the story of brotherly love. Two brothers are reunited due to one's incurable disease. They are almost opposites except for one thing – they both have a passion for bicycling. Costner plays a successful doctor, but his younger brother David, played by David Grant, is a college drop-out. Marcus is serious; David is happy-go-lucky. Suddenly, their father dies and Marcus becomes worried that the same fate (he died of an aneurism) may affect his brother. As a result, he is determined to see him win a cycling race before he dies. Time is the key factor because the brothers must learn to understand each other before death cuts their relationship short. Marcus sees a bicycle as all that he has missed in life. David sees it as the perfect symbol for his carefree nature. A photograph from their past shows Marcus trying to pull David along in a red wagon. He is still trying to pull his brother along, yet, the two have a shared tension from being shy at revealing their feelings. David, at one point resenting the "instant" understanding from his brother, shouts, "What are you trying to do, be a one-minute brother?"

Screenwriter Steve Tesich (who already won an Oscar for his *other* bicycle film, *Breaking Away*) manages to connect the emotions in bicycle racing with those of brotherly love. The screenplay is sensitive enough to allow the brothers to express their love for each other by the film's end without making us drown in tears. The movie really gets moving when David is convinced by Marcus to enter the Coors International Bicycle Classic. John Badham's skill as an action director is fully utilized here. The difficult to endure race takes place over mountainous Colorado terrain. Badham's direction gives the race a palpable energy, but he expertly slows it down to reveal sensitivities and emotions between the two brothers. As film critic and screenwriter Richard Sean Lyon says of Badham's direction: "John Badham is the contemporary equivalent of the solid Hollywood craftsmen like Henry Hathaway and Raoul Walsh. Like them, John Badham can't save a misconceived film – but he won't ruin a good one either. A solid, reliable pro." Badham's earlier successes were much bigger than *American Flyers*. He directed *Saturday Night Fever*, *Blue Thunder* and *WarGames*. *WarGames* was a hit film grossing more than $75 million in the US and Canada alone, but Costner still felt no regrets over leaving that film for his edited out part in Kasdan's *Chill*.

During the filming, Steve Tesich recalls he was thrilled that Costner was able to perform athletically. He also is impressed by the "decent" way in which Costner reacts towards women. As Tesich relates: "I saw him in a bar once, saw him leaning on the bar, and I've never seen anyone look better leaning on a bar. Men tend to be very guarded with other men. He's not, and I'm not, and that's why we get along so well. A guy knows where a guy is coming from. You know Kevin has worked with his hands. He's not afraid of hard work and sweat. You know he has been in sports by the way he walks, by the way his body moves, the way he can relax. You know there is a wonderful appreciation of women that is not lecherous or neurotic." During the early days of getting to know each other Costner and Tesich would bicycle together. He remembers his first ride in Griffith Park in Los Angeles with the young actor: "Kevin really wanted to beat me. This was no small, inner desire, but really out front. I wanted to be on top. I had to beat him, and I did. Why? It was my sport... and my script."

The film was not a success. Costner recalls that, "After the makers of *American Flyers* had taken out everything that mattered to the film, I had to take solace in the kind words of strangers who told me the tragedy touched their lives. It was one small speck of gold that made me go down the river farther." He also had negative words to say about the script changes the meddling hands of director Badham wrought: "I was in love with Tesich's script but not about Badham's directing. I believe in the Western ethic. I believe your word is your bond. I'll do anything for a director who promises he won't make me look foolish. I'll *risk* looking foolish knowing he won't let me." Regardless of the films failure, Costner and Tesich remained close. "Kevin is a nice guy, like a sixties nice guy. He's right out of that period to me – essentially comfortable with all the things that used to stand for 'being a man.' I'm positive of that."

Unlike Tesich's other bicycling film, *American Flyers* was not a hit. The film barely grossed $2 million in US and Canadian ticket sales. Costner had now been in three films which had only earned this amount or less at the box-office: *Stacy's Knights, Fandango* and *American Flyers*. Other young hopefuls should take note that a disappointing box-office does not always mean the end of a career – especially if one is a beginning actor. It is only later, as a full-blown star, with enormous budgets and complete responsibility for a project that one cannot fail. Lawrence Kasdan's *Silverado* was waiting in the wings for Costner, and, as soon as Costner came to the screen in his rowdy cowboy performance as Jake his problems of being a struggling actor began to disappear.

"I knew I would do a Western, just like I would be an actor," says Costner. He even dedicated his performance as Jake in *Silverado* to "everyone who ever dreamed of being in a Western." Ever since his childhood heroes protected the West, Costner had yearned to be in a Western. He really feels he is a man born too late, a man who would have been more comfortable in Dodge City with his gun and his horse, than in Hollywood with his Bronco. Since he was so motivated and enthusiastic about being in a Western, Costner went above and beyond the usual requirements of someone with the size of role and involvement he had in the film. He came to the set on his off days. He kept the cast and crew in stitches by repeating "just about every famous line from every famous Western," remembers one cast member. He has a sense of pure, unadulterated joy at appearing in a Western and this was infectious. About his feelings at the time, he stated simply, "I've waited all my life to do a Western."

The film was based on an original screenplay by Lawrence Kasdan and Mark Kasdan. The stars of *Silverado* were not as well known as they are today, but even then the cast list read like a "Who's Who" of up and coming hot talent: Kevin Kline, Scott Glenn, Rosanna Arquette, John Cleese, Brian Dennehy, Danny Glover, Jeff Goldblum, Linda Hunt, and, of course, Kevin Costner. The plot tells the story of four unwilling heroes who are drawn together by circumstances on their way to Silverado. Instead of Silverado being the harbor of refuge they think it will be, it ends up representing a threat to them. As a result, they can only overcome the danger by forming their unlikely alliance.

Columbia Pictures released this Lawrence Kasdan directed and produced film from the Kasdan brother's original screenplay. Charles Okun and Michael Grillo were executive producers. The film received mixed reviews and, even though it made more than $34 million in US and Canadian box-office receipts, the film still failed to return its cost from this alone (reports of the budget were set at $24+ million). Richard Sean Lyon reports that Kasdan's main problem with directing is that he is not sure whether he wants to please the mass audience or massive groups of critics. Lyon notes in **The 1990 Survival Guide To Film**: "All of Lawrence Kasdan's films have fallen short of their potential because he can't decide if he's writing to entertain – or to win awards. His talents will allow him to choose either route, and the outcome will depend on whether he's more interested in reaching an audience or impressing the critics – it is no longer possible to do both with any consistency for more than five years at a time. (At least not until you're dead – then you're forgiven everything – even success)." Lyon believes that critics resent mass audience success because they feel box-office success immediately symbolizes that the film is just mindless, escapist entertainment.

Even though the film was not a smash hit, Costner was thrilled with his role as Jake, Emmet's daredevil and usually reckless brother. He said at the time he believed Jake would be "one of the greatest characters I'll ever play." He then went into his reasons for wanting to work with *Raiders Of The Lost Ark* scripter Kasdan: "I had very strong feelings about Larry Kasdan after reading an article on him in the Los Angeles Times' Calendar," he says. The article said something along the lines of, "Director hot but has no credits." Costner realized it could have been his own advertisement: "Kevin's hot but he has no films." It would be three years later until Costner found himself in a small role in John Badham's *WarGames*.

However, as already noted, Kasdan was making a film called *The Big Chill*, and, as a result, Badham graciously released Costner from his contract. "Working with Larry on *The Big Chill* was the single biggest move in my career," Costner said then. As to his favor in returning to give Costner another role, the star said, "That's something that's between us." However, he does admit that being cut from the film did upset his loved ones more than himself. "My wife and parents were bummed out, but it didn't bother me. I knew I was in the right film with the right group of people. I knew that I was in, and nobody could ever take that away from me."

Kasdan remembers feeling guilty about Costner's *Chill* scenes. "I dropped the section he was in," recalls the director, "and felt I owed this amazing young actor a part." As they wrote their next script after *The Big Chill*, the Kasdans kept thinking of Costner as they wrote. They wanted someone like him in *Silverado* because "he has energy, lightness, speed, and, at the same time, intensity. I wanted the Jake character to have that kind of untamed energy, the reckless, forward movement that has always attracted me to Westerns."

Costner was enthusiastic to reporters and anyone who would listen concerning his upcoming cowboy role. "*Silverado* has everything you might imagine. To be on horses, to be with a bunch of guys and to shoot guns. It was great fun." It was also extremely cold. The shooting occurred in winter and early spring in Santa Fe, New Mexico. Costner was freezing and had trouble shooting his guns from his hands being so cold. He was only able to do it once because his hands were so cold they wouldn't function. "The scenes where I'm spinning my guns," he explains, "it was hovering around zero." At this point in time, Costner still had very little experience riding a horse. As a result, he and the rest of the cast went to Santa Fe four weeks before the shoot was supposed to commence. The time was spent learning how to ride and how to "mess" with guns, Costner shares. The second half of the day was spent working on the script and its action.

There was a very difficult scene to shoot during this film. There is a huge shoot-out and stampede at MacKendrick's (an evil land baron) ranch. Costner recalls the difficulties experienced during that scene, it sounds almost as if he is explaining his own difficulties years later, trying to direct his buffalo stamped for *Dances With Wolves*. As he recalled the difficult shot: "That was one thing that put us into a bind. We had to spend 11 days shooting it because the stampede wouldn't work out. It lengthened the whole thing. The cows wouldn't cooperate. They were real jerks."

The release of *Silverado* immediately started gaining Costner recognition, but not always of the kind for which he was looking. The media started to hang the label of "sex-symbol" on him and Costner found himself taking exception to this idea. As he states, "I personally don't think I'm that sexy. I see guys that I think are classically handsome and know why a woman likes them. But I don't see myself that way. I can't live up to the media's expectations. I can't and won't be dictated to by what they say." Still, Costner's performance of party-time Jake had red-blooded women writhing in their seats, something for which he was unprepared. He thought he was just playing a "cowboy." "I was lookin' to play a cowboy and I was lookin' to have fun, but I never thought women would respond to it. I guess it's a mothering instinct. They want to take this guy home or something."

Admiring female fans would probably love to know that at one point, earlier on in his life, Costner was quite a reckless lover. "I never dated the same girl twice. My affairs were very short-lived. You couldn't even call them affairs. They were like collisions," he reports. This promiscuity was abruptly halted when he left college and married his sweetheart, Cindy Silva. Costner was very honest about expressing himself where Cindy is concerned. "If the situations were reversed," he says, "I would never handle it as well as she has done. Cindy and I don't have it better than anybody else. We struggle and we work things out, and it's not all dandy." As to his small cult following from this period, Costner relates: "Girls don't run after me. But sometimes guys'll stop me on the street and introduce their girlfriends. They don't seem to be threatened by me, for some weird reason. And they'll say to their girl, 'Hey, this is the guy you liked in that movie!'"

The pressures of success were beginning to gnaw ever so slightly at the psyche of the young actor. "I haven't changed," he insisted. "I'm still able to appreciate each new thing that happens in my life. I mean, the first time a limo came up, my wife and I came out and took pictures of it. Our neighbors came and took pictures, too. And we stood in front of it and posed. The first time we flew first class, we called our parents and told them about the meal they gave us on the flight. I've had a chance to enjoy my life in a way I never thought that I would, and I'm not gonna let these things slip by me."

Speaking of not letting things slip by him, true to his word, Costner would remain basically this "in-awe" individual. For example, Costner was going to see *Silverado* for his fifth time. Everybody on the block where he and Cindy live got together and pulled their resources to hire a babysitter. They then drove the more than thirty miles to a Westwood theater to see the film. They took up an entire row in the theater and the neighbors were thrilled when they saw their friend's name and image hit the screen. As Costner tells the story: "I live in this real middle-class little neighborhood. I get out in my front yard with my Weed Eater, and people stop by with their baby carriages. My neighbors just couldn't believe it when my name went on the screen. They didn't want to go to sleep that night; they just wanted to talk about it."

No matter how "normal" or "middle-class" Costner might view himself, the reality was his life was changing in major ways. One interviewer relates a story in which Costner is being hampered at a social function by his on-screen image. As "US" reported the story: "A young woman, a tall blonde, drifts up and shouts: 'Are you an Untouchable?' She is inches from his face. Costner stoically, instinctively draws himself in, scanning the room over her head with a glazed look of resignation. He stuffs one hand deep inside a pocket and presses his drink against his chest. He is, of course, civil, amusing. He does not want to offend, but he doesn't want to indulge either. He is, it seems, an Uncomfortable. Her boyfriend apologizes, introduces himself, shakes his hand. 'This man was in *Silverado* too,' he explains. Then, aping Costner's dazzling gunplay in the film's finest moment, the boyfriend fires two fist guns into the air, Jake-like, yelling, 'Ka-*boom*, you shot two guys, right?' Right. Costner smiles without opening his mouth. 'I'm cuttin' out,' he says, leaving his glass on the bar as he moves away."

This invasion of privacy might not bother some Hollywood actors who expect it as a part of their career decision, but Costner tries hard to remain to himself – very much as out of the Hollywood spotlight as he can off-screen. Costner admits he saw the "lead romantic" roles coming his way. However, he also says there is no one who does not wonder how this sexual notoriety has affected his wife. "Anybody close to us wonders what Cindy's thinking. It's like Tracy and Hepburn or the definitive love story, *The Way We Were*, where you create this incredible chemistry onscreen. And the woman you live with is sitting there at home shaking her head going, 'No, *we* have the greatest love story.' And it's hard for her to compete. Cindy's getting stronger about it now. She once said, 'What bothers me is that people are going to think you have the woman of everyone's dreams [from his film roles] – and I'm really the woman, right?' And she is right." Rumors of their difficulties would continue from this time onward, though, gossip about Costner's love life rarely reaches print. Still, the trials and tribulations of his continued success and his smash hits, *Robin Hood: Prince of Thieves*, and *Dances With Wolves*, would make Costner behave quite atypically during his London location work for *Prince of Thieves*. That was yet to come however.

Costner was realistic enough about the pressures of success to admit he needed to work overtime to ensure his career didn't affect his marriage and family. He understands that Cindy Silva had no idea when she met, fell in love with, and married him, that she was taking on all the excessive baggage that can result when your husband is a sex-symbol superstar. "You have to modify and monitor these things to keep your life together. I try not to beat myself up over them 'cause I do that enough anyway. It would make my life a lot easier if these things were not there. They aren't that dark or problematic. Given this life style, it makes it harder and harder. I would really be disappointed with myself if our relationship blew up – if I couldn't do these films and keep my marriage together. Cindy didn't marry into all that. I wasn't an actor ten years ago. There's a great risk and we're going to have to fight it." Nonetheless, the pressures were just beginning at this point, and, for the time being, the Costner's were swept up in the success of Kevin's role as Jake in *Silverado*.

One amusing incident occurred when Costner appeared at the Venice Film Festival for the showings of *Fandango* and *Silverado*. One morning he was in the Excelsior bar getting a little pissed. As he was drinking he looked up and saw Mel Gibson enter the bar. Gibson was also intent on getting a little pissed and the two started drinking. They decided after a knocking a few back to go for a ride. As Costner remembers, they decided to borrow a couple of locked bikes and go for a spin: "We went outside, and they were all locked. So Mel went off and found one, but not two. I said I'd ride; I'd just done this bike picture. And it was great. There we were, on Lido Island, and Mel's on the goddamned handlebars looking like E.T.! I even think there was a full moon."

Costner constantly professes to be awkward with his sex-symbol image, feelings backed up by both his directors in the baseball films he would come to lead in, *Bull Durham* and *Field Of Dreams*, directed by Ron Shelton and Phil Alden Robinson respectively. As Shelton says of Costner's reluctance, "he slips in and out of crowds very quietly, without making a scene, and seems slightly embarrassed by it." Phil Alden Robinson proclaims that "Costner is a guy who women find attractive and men are not put off by. He never has to resort to being weird." Still, Costner's nice-guy performances that include a little bit of toughness, sex and fun continued to endear him to legions of female fans the world round.

As much as he appreciates the talent and skills of writer/director/producer Kasdan, Costner's reputation for being a driven, meddling perfectionist came to the fore anyway. As Kasdan stated, "In practically every scene he was opinionated about what he could do. He's like a well, always coming up with ideas, but I couldn't listen to 10 ideas every time. I had to get my brother to act as a filter." Marilyn Vance, costume designer on *The Untouchables* backs up this image of Costner: "He asks a million questions. He doesn't make it easy on anyone, nor on himself." John Badham also experienced the frustrations that come about by trying to handle all of Costner's on-set enthusiasm and energy: "His mind is working all the time. 'What about if I do this?' 'How 'bout if I said such and such?' Ninety percent of the time it was an improvement, but it was almost a relief to get him on the bicycle."

Countless others have given this picture of Costner, and even solid professionals like De Palma insist there are few people around as obsessed with their work as Costner. Says the defendant, "You have to be an emotional detective when it comes to playing your part. If you haven't been paying attention, or you're shooting out of continuity, and you haven't found out what they're doing – well, I get pissed off when I miss things like that." De Palma did come to Costner's defense somewhat by explaining why he added so much to his future role of Eliot Ness: "Kevin doesn't have a phoney bone in his body. He has a lot of terribly unsophisticated lines to say about the law, and the right – 'We've got to be pure,' he says at one point – and he makes this stuff work because of his innate purity, which is the same essence as Eliot Ness. Kind of a white knight in a cesspool. Kevin grows in the movie. He goes from this simple Candide character to one as close to Dirty Harry as you can get," and still ring true to the character of Eliot Ness. Costner was also growing from his ever-burgeoning career demands. After seeing him in *Silverado*, audiences and producers only wanted more, much more.

What the critics said about
Fandango, American Flyers & Silverado:

FANDANGO
Director- Kevin Reynolds

In PEOPLE (Irma Velasco)
"Screenwriter-director Kevin Reynolds, a Steven Spielberg protege, makes his feature debut with this intermittently funny movie about five Texas frat brats who finish college in 1971 and decide it's time for an inebriated pilgrimage across the desert.... Kevin Costner is the group's leader – a con man who can no longer avoid a draft notice. Costner does seem as if he could talk a riled-up ratler out of his fangs – he has an easy charm and, for a Southern California native, a not-too-affected Texas twang.... Things get downright sappy too: Costner dreams about a young blonde romping in a field of purple wildflowers. FANDANGO'S real problem is that it doesn't know what to be – a love story? an antiwar statement? a socially conscious ANIMAL HOUSE II Stranded in the desert, Costner drawls, "Going nowhere in the privilege of youth." It is not, however, a privilege long afforded to young movie directors."

AMERICAN FLYERS
Director – John Badham

In MACLEANS (Lawrence O'Toole)
"AMERICAN FLYERS is extremely affecting and likable, in part because it deals with characters who, underneath rather ordinary veneers, exhibit deeper qualities... Badham knows how to slow down for the film's more sensitive moments and it is a tribute to both him and writer Steve Tesich [recipient of the Oscar for script of 1979s BREAKING AWAY] that such scenes never become cloying.... AMERICAN FLYERS is a modern rarity – a writer's movie. It expresses one man's powerful personal vision.... Without drowning in tears, AMERICAN FLYERS touches some tender spots in its gentle depiction of two of the most intimate strangers."

In NEWSWEEK (David Ansen)
"It's tempting to dismiss AMERICAN FLYERS as the most shamelessly manipulative movie of the season. It combines two of the wettest ploys of the era: the win-one-for-the-gipper athletic competition (in this case, bicycle racing) and the herditary-disease-strikes-down-youth gambit. The latter is spiced with the teasing ambiguity of which of two brothers is going to bite the dust – Marcus (Kevin Costner), the doctor who would have been a racing contender, or the boyish Davy (David Grant), who needs to find his dream and Prove Himself.

The exasperating thing is that writer Steve Tesich (who already wrote the bicycle movie, BREAKING AWAY) and director John Badham (SATURDAY NIGHT FEVER) are no hacks: the details and dialogue are consistently superior to the sappy themes. So is the quietly powerful Costner, who proves that his SILVERADO flash was not in the pan."

SILVERADO
Director – Lawrence Kasdan

In TIME (Richard Corliss)
"Now there's SILVERADO, the Cuisinart western! Silverado dices, splices, chops, co-opts, hones and clones every oater archetype in just 2 hr 13 min .; that's less than 1% of the time it would take you to sit through the collected works of John Wayne! And if you act now, we'll throw in nine, yes, nine of the cinema's rising stars –
Kevinklinescottglennrosannaarquettejohncleesekevincostner briandennehydannygloverjeffgoldblumandlindahunt
– almost none of whom look at home on the range. As screenwriter (RAIDERS OF THE LOST ARK) and writer-director (BODY HEAT), Lawrence Kasdan has performed deft surgery on the Saturday-matinee serial and the film noir melodrama. But the western will not yield."

In THE NEW REPUBLIC (Stanley Kauffmann)
"SILVERADO is like an overstuffed deli sandwich – discouraging rather than prodigal. Not a sandwich at all, really: a big pile of meat with token and irrelevant pieces of bread at either end. My procedure – many do it, the counterman tells me – is to buy two extra slices of bread, take all the stuff home, and make two sandwiches, bite-size, manageable, not a jaw chore.

If only you could do something like that with SILVERADO, you might come up with two tolerable 70-minute films. As is, it's grossly overstuffed – with lots of plots (not really interwoven strands), lots of stock characters and stock scenes, and lots – I mean lots – of symphony-size music."

In THE NEW YORKER (Pauline Kael)
"Lawrence Kasdan is an impersonal craftsman, hip in a post-modern way that's devoid of personality. He uses accomplished actors: the four heroes journeying west to Silverado in the eighteen-eighties are played by Kevin Kline, Scott Glenn, Kevin Costner, and Danny Glover, and they're variously involved with Linda Hunt, Rosanna Arquette, Brian Dennehy, John Cleese, and Jeff Goldblum. But these actors don't seem sure what their characters are meant to be, and though I kept waiting for the four men's stories to converge and the villains to turn out to be linked, as far as I could see, this didn't happen."

PART
2
THE FILMS

CHAPTER

4

THE UNTOUCHABLES
& NO WAY OUT

The *Untouchables* is the film that shot Kevin Costner to instant recognition and stardom. Even though Costner spent 10 years trying to achieve stardom, this film had everyone acting as if, overnight, Costner had made it.

Producer Art Linson never had any doubts about Costner and knew from the beginning that he was Eliot Ness. Said Linson, "There was no doubt in my mind that Kevin was the best for it. I wanted him as soon as I saw *Silverado*. He looked like a great Midwestern movie star to me – a very classic leading man with a Gary Cooper feel to him. I thought Eliot Ness had to be a true-blue American. Even if Mel Gibson fixed his accent, there'd be something missing. Paramount was nervous: Kevin wasn't famous. So what we did was surround him with people who were."

Famous people indeed. The cast of *The Untouchables* were among the finest actors he has worked with in his career. Sean Connery, Robert DeNiro and Andy Garcia all gave terrific performances, with Connery and DeNiro two consummate actors battling each other on opposite teams of good and evil.

As Pauline Kael noted, "The Disney moviemakers knew that Snow White alone would be stupefying; she needed the Seven Dwarfs. And Mamet and De Palma know that the way to set off the Waspy-white Eliot Ness, the family man, is to surround him with misfits who are unlike him in everything except loyalty, courage, and a belief in justice "

To ensure he would stand up to the competition, Costner, already dedicated to perfecting his characterizations, doubled up on his homework. He read every book he could find that concerned itself with the Twenties and Thirties, Prohibition, breweries and bootleggers. He and his wife toured all the sites in the film, pouring over photos of buildings, taxis and bulletproof vests owned by the Chicago Historical Society. The widow of one of Capone's lieutenants was still alive and Costner shared her reminiscences about the "old days."

Costner is known to be obsessive about accuracy and he didn't stop here. Adolph Brown had been a clerk in Ness' office and the actor spoke with him several times and Bob Feusel, president of the Federal Criminal Investigators Association. From his time spent, he learned how to hold a .38 and .45 and how much kickback to count on. He also learned that a gun was never pulled unless it was going to be used.

Costner even met with Al Wolff, an 88 year old who was actually one of the original "Untouchables." Wolff proved to be a gold mine of valuable information.

Wolff, known as "Wallpaper" because that was the only thing he left in speakeasies when he shut them down, helped form the 1929 crime team headed by Ness. The two worked together until 1933, and Wolff helped coach Costner in his role as Ness.

"We were all tough guys, I guess," Wolff recalled. "Eliot Ness was young like me when I first met him. He became a tough guy, but a tough guy with class. He was naive when he started, but he learned. He got a little rougher 'cause it got a little dangerous."

Wolff was even able to share with Costner his first and only meeting with Capone. As he recalled, "I met Capone only once, in Hot Springs, Arkansas. I was still working for Ness at the time, but I was on vacation. I had already blown my cover by going to testify in court. Capone came over to me, and he says, 'Oh, so you're Wolff. I heard nice things about ya.' See, I was a maverick agent. I would never take a place without a warrant. I never violated a law to enforce one.

"So Capone says, 'I understand you never framed anybody. You let them make bond. You're a nice fella. I wish I had guys like you working for me.' I said, 'You can't have me; I'll live longer.'

"The papers used to write him up all the time. They called him a Robin Hood, and everybody knew he used to give baskets to poor people at Christmas time. I never saw him kill anybody. Forget about the movie; the movie is Hollywood. Personally, Capone seemed all right with me. But when I met him, I said I didn't condone what he was doing," he recalled.

According to Wolff, Costner's performance of Eliot Ness was superior to the role played by Robert Stack in the television series based on Ness' memoirs.

As Wolff calls it, "Robert Stack was nowhere near as good as Kevin Costner in acting like Ness. He was rough from the start. When the movie people took me out of the closet to show Costner how to act like Ness, I told him how to walk. Ness walked slowly. And I showed Costner how to use the gun. I said, 'When you take a gun out, be ready to use it, because it's your life or their life.' Parts of this was pretty real, but there was also a lot of Hollywood that they had to put in it. But I enjoyed the movie. Costner did a good job. I was a good teacher. "

One interesting side note to the Al Wolff story is that, until the producers contacted him, not even his own family had been aware of his involvement with Ness during the late Twenties and early Thirties.

The making of *The Untouchables* goes back almost two

years before its release. Producer Art Linson and Paramount's Ned Tanen, president of the Motion Picture group, were having a business breakfast and Tanen talked about trying to buy the rights to 'The Untouchables' television series. So, when Linson mentioned he wanted to give 'The Untouchables' a brushing off, Tanen was enthusiastic.

However, Linson had some doubts. As he recalls, "I didn't want to do a remake or a sequel and I didn't want to do a spoof. I wanted to create a big-scale movie about mythical American heroes."

Brian De Palma was set to direct the film from a screenplay by David Mamet, who took the assignment as his first writing job after winning the Pulitzer Prize for his Broadway play, "Glengarry, Glen Ross."

Linson had to wine and dine Mamet before convincing him that it would be good for his career to follow up his Broadway success with 'The Untouchables' screenplay. As Linson relates, "It took a little wheedling."

"'Don't you think the logical career move would be to do a remake of a TV series?', I asked him," Linson remembered. "Sure," answered Mamet before Linson had to do any more cajoling. "The Untouchables" television series ran from 1959 to 1963 and included a septet introduced by the rat-a-tat-tat voice-over of Walter Winchell. Half-lit grey tones were used to shoot the series, which ran for an hour and had a then-shocking body count at the end of each episode. The show finally was knocked off the air when it came up against the hit show, "Sing Along With Mitch."

After watching the two-hour original show of the television "Untouchables," Mamet decided that "it was beautiful but there was nothing I could use for the movie. I had to write an original story. The way Al Capone was caught was not very dramatic," he said of the gangster, who was ultimately convicted for evasion of income tax.

Linson convinced De Palma to do the film after showing him the third draft of the script. De Palma was getting tired of making the suspense thrillers sprinkled with heavy doses of violence that had built his reputation. When he read the script, he immediately wanted to do it.

"What was different for me about *The Untouchables* was that I found myself caring a lot more about the characters," he said. "With a suspense movie, the point had been just to shock people. I never saw it as a gangster movie. I saw it more as a 'Magnificent Seven'."

The ordeals involved in trying to sign the rest of the "quality" cast to support Costner reads like a handbook on the problems associated with casting a feature film in Hollywood. The first chore was casting Sean Connery to play Malone, the Irish cop with the proverbial "heart of gold" and one of the few officers not on Capone's payroll.

Linson hesitated before trying to get Connery because he "couldn't imagine going to his agent, Mike Ovitz, and saying, 'We want Sean Connery to play a supporting role to Kevin Costner – and by the way, we can't pay him much money."

Still, that's exactly the way it happened. When Connery read the script, he couldn't help but relish a good fight with Capone's "baroque Mediterranean mind, running with all that Italian built-in Machiavellianism – and the whole police force in his pocket."

Connery agreed to do the role for a low fee but against a percentage of the take (a decision that turned out to be quite shrewd). Connery had a secret admiration for De Palma's work and was interested in taking a chance on the director. "I'd seen his films, so I agreed to take a chance on a piece of it. He has a marvelous technical sense, a nice sense of style, and he's quite fearless in the way he goes in whatever direction he takes," Connery said.

"I liked elements of his films always, [but] my feeling was that they were a bit too detached. And then when we talked, I was very aware what he was attempting to do – I see how much he is using the kind of emotional colors of the parts... how well he's conceived the human elements... I think the emotional level of the story will surprise many people," added Connery.

The filming was problematic due to inclement weather and the busy Chicago city traffic. Costner was frequently frustrated because he was only be able to do his scenes when the traffic controllers would allow it and would spend down time walking six inches from the edges of rooftops on 120 feet high buildings to prepare for his roof-top "eye-for-an-eye" murder scene near the end of the film.

With the poor weather causing shooting delays, De Palma and Linson were soon feeling glum. That left Connery and Costner on the set for comedy relief. Costner started doing one of his favorite shticks – ad-libbing Paul Newman and Richard Boone in "Hombre." "You got a lot of bark on you, Mister," he says in his best raspy Boone voice. "What do you suppose hell looks like?" Costner had been quite unaware of the fact that Connery's ex-wife Diane Cilento was the tempting pioneer woman in the same film. "Who was that woman, anyway?" Costner asked at one point. "That was my wife," says Connery, with a twinkle in his eye and a naughty James Bond grin spreading across his lips.

"That was your wife?" said the incredulous Costner.

"That's great. Jeez, Sean, you're something." Nervous cast members began to look into the sky for some sign that the inclement weather would let up.

Next to be signed to the picture was young actor Andy Garcia, assigned to the role of Stone, Ness's Italian-American sharpshooter. Then came Charles Martin Smith, who took the role of Oscar Wallace, the accountant-turned-fighter. Connery offered support and guidance to all three young actors, much as he was to do for the Ness character as written. "We determined before that I was going to take them – onstage and offstage – under my wing," Connery explained.

Connery has defended the movie by saying, "The movie isn't a fairy tale, it's true." The underdog victorious over the bully is really the theme of the movie, which is why many feel Costner's performance of Ness as a man who only slowly comes to realize he must use violence to enforce the law is accurate.

A stickler for details when it comes to the script, Costner comments on his innovations to the Ness character. "I get up in the middle of the night and make notes about things like, 'I don't want to have my jacket on here. Why don't I want to have my jacket on *here*?

"For *The Untouchables*, I started making newspaper clippings and had the prop guy put them on a board to show my progress as Ness – 'Ness Busts Out,' 'War Of Words Begins, Ness and Capone,' 'Ness Will Never Make It," he recalled.

"I really like to work with the best people possible, but I'm never, ever going to work on something just because I want to work with somebody," he said of the stellar cast he worked with. "I have to work with them when the script's right. I would do five Westerns in a row if they were five great scripts."

However, Costner forgot his own advice when he later chose to do *Robin Hood: Prince of Thieves*. While the film would be a box-office hit, Costner decided to do it because friend Kevin Reynolds was directing. The film would mark the breaking point of their friendship and would be what Costner described as his "least satisfying film artistically."

Costner has many times heard accusations that his performance as Eliot Ness was too white-bread. This was, after all, an Eliot Ness that promises his wife he'll be "careful as mice" while chasing Capone, and receives notes from his wife in his lunch bag telling him how proud she is of his efforts .

As Costner relates, "A reporter once said to me, 'I think Eliot Ness is a wimp.' And I said, 'Did you see the movie? What you're saying is that this guy is not a classic hero, but did you ever see him ever take a step backwards? Ever?'" Costner believes that because Ness does not fit into the stereotypical definition of hero does not mean he is not one.

He cautions, "You see a guy like that, like Eliot Ness, has a family and stuff, and it doesn't match up to the archetype of a real strong guy." However, it's no wonder some would find Ness a bit too "kind" and "gentle," especially since he is depicted chomping on carrot sticks and riding around in a snowplow while shouting to his team, "Let's do some good."

Speaking of strong guys, the tides of ego and genius became a serious consideration for Art Linson and Paramount studios when casting the pivotal role of Al Capone. De Palma wanted DeNiro, known for his perfectionism and compulsory attention to details. However,

Paramount became nervous and wasn't sure it was worth the $1.5 million is was going to cost them for the two weeks it would take DeNiro to perform his part. Eventually, Paramount conceded.

The original budget, which had been set at $17 million, soon swelled to $24 million before the filming was over. *Amadeus* designer Patrizia von Brandenstein recreated a whole block of LaSalle Street, including 125 torpedoes and over 60 vintage cars. Due to Capone's control, the streets were kept immaculate. Interestingly enough, De Palma says his conception of corruption was that "it's very clean."

The director had hoped to have a period train also, but when penny-pinching executives discovered it was going to cost $200,000, they said no. De Palma instead improvised, using Union Station to film his final scene, modeled after the Odessa Steps scene in Sergei Eisenstein's "Battleship Potemkin." As Linson recalls, De Palma just said, "Okay, guys, we've run out of money. Give me a staircase, a clock and a baby carriage."

Once DeNiro was hired, he lived up to his reputation for perfectionism and attention to detail. He explained that the Sicilian Italian he played in *The Godfather II* was different than the Neapolitan Italian of Capone: "The Sicilian is a darker personality, closer to Africa. The Neapolitans are more lively and flamboyant."

Similar to his role in "Raging Bull," DeNiro gained 25 pounds for the part of Al Capone by wolfing down pasta, milkshakes and anything else he could to make himself heavier. DeNiro found that "gaining the weight was hard, very hard and depressing. It's the last time I'll ever do that."

DeNiro used plugs to broaden his nose and had his hairline reshaped to simulate the Capone dome. According to DeNiro, "It sounds simple, but it took a week, sitting in a barber's chair for seven hours at a stretch while they snipped and shaved and tweezed, checking with photographs of Capone. It was incredible. If just one hair was off, it looked artificial."

DeNiro also had an entire wardrobe designed, using the same maker of silk underwear that Capone had. For hours at a time, he would test different suits, shirts, overcoats and even different sizes of cigars before the camera. Most would consider this attention to detail a mania if it were not combined with the talent of DeNiro. As Linson says, "Bob has earned a right to do all that."

Before getting DeNiro, Paramount had signed Bob Hoskins (*Who Framed Roger Rabbit?*) to the role. However, Linson pushed for DeNiro and finally got him. It was a fortuitous sign for Costner that, while he may have been the one surrounded by all this established talent, his name read first in the credits.

Costner found working with De Palma the one time when he was a little intimidated by his director, but he discovered his fears were unfounded. "Brian always had an ear for me. Never when I asked Brian something would he be irritated. Never would I ask him and he wouldn't have an answer," he said.

"In the film, I have a little girl and I'm putting her to bed and I wanted to try to develop a routine with her. You know, a Daddy routine: a kiss and then a butterfly kiss and then an Eskimo kiss, because we're going to have a scene where we're torn from each other's arms and I'm separated from my family. So I start to do it and the other actors say, 'What are you doing?' But Brian totally understood. Whether he agreed with me or not, he didn't shit all over what I had to say. Maybe he didn't even like it. But he embraced it," recalls Costner.

Costner was overwhelmed by being on the same set as Connery and DeNiro. He realized he was in the "major leagues" with these two actors and tried to absorb all he could from the experience.

"Both DeNiro and Connery are keen collaborators," says Costner. "If you even mention something to them, their eyes get real big and their ear comes to you – they wanna know. What makes them great is that, if nobody else doesn't know, they know."

Costner also felt that Ness should be played as Malone's alter ego. "My challenge," he says, "is to make people like a person who takes a moral stance, who for the first twenty minutes may seem to be a dope, a bore. The challenge is to make people like me. I don't look for the big bite – 'Okay, now are you on my side?' – I'm just looking for the ugliness to surface and then for people to look around and say, 'Who is gonna deal with this? Who's equipped and who's willing?' The thing is, maybe Eliot's not even equipped – but he's willing."

For a while, Costner was worried that the way Mamet, De Palma and Al Wolff had told him to play Eliot Ness was wrong. He felt the steely image that Robert Stack had created in the television role was being undermined. "Could I fight it?" he remembers wondering. "Could I win the audience by the end of the movie? It's a big hole to climb out of."

Mamet and De Palma listened patiently to their star and then assured him he was wrong. Costner now says, "They were right. People are always saying they don't want another Rambo. Well, here's Eliot Ness. He doesn't have all the answers. He doesn't do his thinking with a gun. He's troubled. He's naive. The critics beg for something different and then, when you give it to them, they don't like it."

However, audiences loved the film's portrayal of Ness as a man who shows no violence except in making a payback. For example, when he kills the man responsible for killing Malone, it is seen as justice – the principle of "an eye for an eye" – because Ness would only act with violence in order for "good" to resurface.

There were, however, creative differences. Mamet does not remember Art Linson or Brian De Palma too fondly. Both Linson and De Palma pressed on for one revision after another of the original script. "Some of the things they wanted I didn't agree with, but most were very helpful," he said.

Mamet did seven versions of the script, with the producer and director pretty much deciding on a final version that retained most of the flavor and spirit of Mamet's original draft. Still, Mamet did comment in *American Film* magazine about the "great and lasting joy it gave me to give [Linson] a simple and dignified, 'Get lost'."

After wrapping up the film's production, Art Linson, on a flight to Los Angeles, happened to look up from his newspaper and glance at his seat companion – television's Eliot Ness, Robert Stack. The two soon fell into conversation.

"The Ness I play wouldn't work in the movie," Stack told Linson. "My Ness is a pot boiling, with the lid flipping on top." When Linson told him that the film depicted a younger, domestic Ness, Stack looked skeptical. Before landing, he patted the young producer on the back and said, "Don't worry. If it does as well for you guys as it has for me, you'll be very, very happy."

The movie, which has grossed over $75 million to date, has made Linson and Paramount very, very happy indeed.

What the critics said about

THE UNTOUCHABLES

In THE NEW YORKER (Pauline Kael)
"Special Agent Eliot Ness (Kevin Costner) is a fresh-faced young innocent who doesn't even understand that bootlegging couldn't flourish without the collaboration of the police, and that the mobsters have bribed the officials, the judges, the mayor. At first, we wonder how anyone could think that this stiff is up to the job (or that Costner is up to playing the role). That's part of the film's plan: Mamet and De Palma want us to recognize that Ness, in his neat gray suit, is too clean to be able to clean up Chicago (and they've worked out how they mean to use Costner's blandness, too)....Ness says at the beginning that he will do anything 'within the law' to destroy Capone's grip on the city; the point of his character is that as he gets to know himself better, he learns he'll do more."

No Way Out

As his next film project following the smash success of *The Untouchables*, Costner chose to do *No Way Out*, a remake of the 1948 Charles Laughton – Ray Milland film *The Big Clock*. The film was another Orion pictures release and Mace Neufeld, Laura Ziskin and Robert Garland produced. Garland also wrote the script from his adaptation of the novel The Big Clock by Kenneth Fearing. The film was directed by Australian Roger Donaldson (*Smash Palace*).

The movie is a sophisticated suspense thriller but as Costner said before its opening, "You're not going to know where this movie goes. I've always enjoyed stories where you think you've got everything figured out – then they spring the trap ."

The film gave Costner a chance to star with the seasoned talent of Gene Hackman as a U.S. Secretary of Defense. His female co-star was Sean Young as a Washington "party" girl. Critic Pauline Kael felt that Hackman's expression conveyed that he did not want to be in the picture and that he hoped "maybe the film would go away." The sexy and striking Sean Young plays Susan Atwill, the mistress everyone wants.

Roger Donaldson wanted to cast Costner in the role of Lt. Commander Tom Farrell after his intense "hell-raising" performance as Jake in *Silverado*. Donaldson believed that "the wild man behind Costner's surfer-boy looks" was exactly what the character required. As Costner noted about his intense involvement: "When I perform, I like to get out of control. Whomever I play, I enter his world. I don't phone it in. But that's what we *do* in movies. We go into other people's worlds. All the way in."

In the film, Costner plays the young naval officer who is assigned to track down a witness who may or may not be a killer or a Soviet agent. The only factor hindering his investigation is that the one crucial witness is missing.

Hackman plays the Secretary of Defense who has a mistress he likes to have present at big Washington functions (at which his wife is also present) so he can keep an eye on her.

When he finds out she has become involved with

another man (it is Farrell, unbeknownst to him), he kills her accidentally during a fight. Hackman's aide must come up with a plan to save him and suggests that they invent a story about a Soviet spy, who can be blamed for the whole incident.

In the end, Costner turns out to be a Soviet intelligence agent whose double identity neatly solves all the story's loose ends and "springs the trap" to which Costner referred earlier. However, this tacked-on and half-credible plot element caused the film to be trashed by the critics.

The film was beautifully captured by John Alcott shortly before he died in an accident just after filming ended. Director Donaldson keeps it in a state of perpetual motion, with the Washington landscapes adding a great deal to the film's elegant and slick look.

From the elegant Embassy Row to the maze-like corridors of the Pentagon, the action is staged in tight spots such as the Pentagon, adding to the film's suspense (much as *Die Hard* possessed added suspense from everyone being trapped in one location) .

The film shows Costner as lover more than hero, but it also shows him as a man of "action" – at least a man *defined* by his actions. The parallels to Contragate and Oliver North are present in the film's plot.

As usual, Costner shocked producers and the insurance company by insisting on doing all his own stunts. For example, the film contains a very dangerous car chase and Costner performed his part in it, even though, as Donaldson found out later, "he can't see a thing without his glasses." This reckless bravado is what makes insurance companies wince and Costner resemble one of the guys who's still trying to prove his "worth."

There was another dangerous stunt in the film that Costner insisted on doing. As Tom Farrell, he has to perform a dangerous sea rescue. Under perilous conditions, Costner performed the stunt himself, to the dismay of onlooking insurance agents.

When asked if there was any pressure for him to stop doing his own stunts now that he was becoming a highly bankable commodity, he replied, "Yep. Doesn't work very well. It's too late now. I put my own restrictions on myself. I don't have a death wish. I won't do something I don't think I can handle or something that doesn't have to be me. But if I can't see anyone doing it better than me then I put myself in the shot. I'm that kind of guy. I'm involved, crazy in my movies. I go for the straight line. I like the smart call in movies."

The constant action of "No Way Out" was something Costner actually looked forward to. His athletic grace and agility are becoming recognized as part of his character. As Costner relates, "Action is something I identify with a lot. If there's anything in my way I'll run through it, I'll jump over it, I'll do what I think the normal guy would do in that situation. You don't leave a gun lying around, you take it with you. If you're running for your life, you don't have a girl who falls on her heel. In smart films she would take her fuckin' shoes off! I am not that fit. If we went out and jogged now, I'd probably collapse after 400 or 500 yards."

The action in the film that had most of Costner's fans talking, however, was the action between Sean Young and him in the back seat of a limousine. Hose, garter belts and undergarments are disposed of so quickly that it is enough to immediately dispel the image of Eliot Ness, family man.

The sex scene was steamy and Sean Young admits it

Photo: Greg Gorman/Gamma Liaison

"The Untouchables" – Paramount Pictures

"No Way Out" – Globe Photos

"Dances With Wolves" – Orion

"Dances With Wolves" – Orion

"Robin Hood" – Rex Features

"Field Of Dreams" – Universal

"Revenge" – Columbia

was difficult for she and Costner to perform such an intimate scene for cast, crew and camera. As she tells it, "Kevin was nervous. The crew was nervous. The director was worried. It wasn't a pleasant experience. It's never fun to reveal your body. I don't care what anyone says. I was sick when I saw my body up there on the screen. I couldn't get over the fact that Mom and my boyfriend were going to see this. We had to do these love scenes in the limo, and finally, we would just turn around and go, 'Cut!' And then it was like, 'All right, I'll sit over here and you sit over there for a while.' We'd give ourselves a break, and then I'd say, 'All right, honey, do up my dress, let's go.'"

Costner mirrors these feelings of uncomfortability in doing love scenes. Of his "Bull Durham" love scene with Susan Sarandon, he said, "I've never been comfortable with them [sex scenes]. You think about them the night before. You don't want to be embarrassed. It's very difficult to get me to take off my shirt. I don't know why. I just feel awkward doing it. I've done it, but I just don't do it at the drop of a hat. I mean, I'm not a prude. You've seen my movies. I always depend on the script. What bothers me more than anything is now everyone knows how I kiss." Costner's demure feelings about disrobing seem sincere. However, his pants seem to come off much easier than his shirt. In his last three films (*Revenge, Dances With Wolves,* and *Robin Hood: Prince of Thieves*), we have been privileged to fully nude buttocks shots of the "uncomfortable" star. Perhaps he feels his best angle is from the rear.

Still, as Young says, "I think he is a little embarrassed by all this sex-symbol stuff. It is sort of a necessary evil. But outside his work, his life is really centered on his family."

No Way Out was not a commercial success for Orion

pictures. The film only grossed approximately $32 million from U.S. and Canadian distribution, not enough to make it a financial success.

However, Costner's love scenes and easy-going charm won him legions of new male and female fans. He was voted the "Star of Tomorrow" after his work in this film and the success of *The Untouchables*.

Costner was definitely becoming a force to be reckoned with in Hollywood. Critics were saying he was the first leading man to become a matinee idol since Harrison Ford, but the actor was not about to limit himself as just another pretty face.

It was soon after this he would begin building his reputation as producer and director.

In TIME (Richard Schickel)
"The final flaw in *No Way Out* (a preposterous plot twist) spoils this lively, intelligent remake of 1948's *The Big Clock*. A naval officer (Kevin Costner) is assigned to investigate a murder committed by his boss, the Secretary of Defense (Gene Hackman), but for which the officer is the prime suspect. Costner and the victim-to-be (gorgeous Sean Young) play a romping, stomping love scene in the backseat of a limousine as if no one had ever heard about sexually communicable diseases.... Why Donaldson and writer Robert Garland chose to sacrifice sympathy for Costner's character (and their well-made movie) by giving him a second, superfluous identity is a mystery infinitely more baffling than the one they have made."

In NATIONAL REVIEW (John Simon)
"It is not the stuff that is being attacked as garbage, glutted

as our screens are with it, that is depressing these days. What truly depresses is the stuff that gets praised by critics who ought to know better.... In *No Way Out*, there is a trick ending that lacks a shred of sense and vitiates whatever credibility and sympathy may have been elicited before. That audiences are willing to sit through this ending without demanding their money back is perhaps even more astounding than a sudden discussion of Russian literature in an otherwise totally anti-intellectual context.... Kevin Costner, the new superstar in the making, struck me as all right as the wild kid brother in the dreadful *Silverado*, and stiff and dullish as Eliot Ness in De Palma's unspeakable *Untouchables*. As Tom Farrell, he leaves me cold again: I don't trust a face with twice as much jaw to it as forehead, and though a gravelly voice can be interesting, a sandy one merely grates. Costner manages somehow to be both loutish and drab – but that may well be what this age craves in its heroes."

In THE NEW YORKER (Pauline Kael)
"No Way Out doesn't have an ounce of credibility, but the director Roger Donaldson whips the action along with camera angles changing so fast you hardly have time to ask what the chases are for or why the story points don't follow through....The actors have almost nothing to work with... You have to keep your eye on the action, which is wherever Kevin Costner is; his peril is what the movie is all about.... The picture, which is told from Costner's point of view, outsmarts itself in a surprise shift that betrays what we've been watching and makes fools of us.... As an eagerly rising young man, Costner has a pleasant air of not thinking too much of himself, and he gives you the impression that he's

doing what's wanted of him. Still, this agile fellow who spends the whole movie in movement is the essence of laid back. He has no inner energy, no kinetic charge."

CHAPTER

5

BULL DURHAM &
FIELD OF DREAMS

Bull Durham is a film that generated a lot of success and sex-symbol imagery for Costner. Costner played Crash Davis, a man who loved baseball even after it failed to love him any longer. After spending 12 years in the minor leagues as a catcher, he's given the position of educating a rookie pitcher with a "million dollar arm and a five-cent brain."

Durham was an Orion Pictures release of a Mount Company production, which co-starred Susan Sarandon and Tim Robbins. Ron Shelton was the movie's director and wrote the dialogue that did much to help build Costner's straight-talking, sex-symbol image. At one point, Crash Davis informs Annie Savoy (Sarandon): "I believe in the small of a woman's back, the hanging curve ball, high flies, good scotch. I believe Lee Harvey Oswald acted alone. I believe there ought to be a constitutional amendment outlawing Astroturf and the designated hitter. And I believe in long, slow, deep, soft, wet kisses that last three days."

Parallelling Costner and his film career, the character cares more about his profession – baseball – than anything in the world. And much like the duality in Costner's character, Crash Davis is hardnosed, shrewd and abrasive, but when he hits the field (makes a movie), he is ten years old again. Indeed, at this point in his career, Costner seemed to portray characters whose psychological make-up was similar to his own. Durham, for example, allows Costner to utilize his athletic background and his early years of struggle as an actor.

"If you're going to enter into anybody else's world, you should do as much as possible to honor it," says the actor. "That's problematic in certain films; in a sports film in particular, you can tell when a guy's not really an athlete."

Being a three-team athlete in high school, Costner had no trouble handling the athletic requirements of the role. Additionally, his empathy with Crash's love for baseball comes from his own struggles while pursuing his love – acting.

He explains the parallel: "What's important to my character is that it wasn't beneath him to play down there in Durham. You see a lot of guys go, 'I'm gonna give this acting thing two, three, five years. If I don't make it in that time, I'm out.' Ballplayers say, 'Just four years in the minor leagues, no more.' Crash, though you may think of him as somewhat pathetic, doesn't give up his dream. He would rather play this game than sell Lady Kenmores, and I find that heroic."

After ten years of struggle before getting his real acting career moving, Costner can certainly relate to risking the nine-to-five security for one's true love – even if one has to risk nearly everything to gain it.

Costner adds a great deal of humanity to Crash, and this makes him much more appealing. The film is a comedy about minor league baseball and second-rate romance. Costner's skill at playing actually lends much more credibility to this film than most baseball pictures exhibit. Where the love interest is concerned, Costner plays it in his usual, no-crap-given-or-taken manner.

Although Costner believes he could have been a professional athlete, he decided against applying himself towards that end. "I could have played farther on," he says. "I just didn't believe it. I never acknowledged in college that I was a really good athlete. Had I chosen baseball over acting, I could have been a player. Everybody I went to high school with is gonna say 'bull.' But if I'd told the people I was gonna be an actor, they'd say 'bull,' too."

Costner remembered his high school classmates in his *Dances With Wolves* acceptance speech. Because of his early transitory years, he never felt like "one of the guys" during his high school years.

Moving around so much made Costner believe he had to impress a whole new crowd of people as he developed new friendships. Because he was a loner, this was not an easy process.

Obviously, Costner never lost the feeling that he was an "outsider" from his high school days or he would not, at age 36 and with 15 films and Oscar and box-office success behind him, worry about what the "kids" from high school would think.

The struggles Crash Davis experiences while trying to remain close to a profession he loves with all his soul reminded Costner of the indignities he often had to suffer while trying to pursue his goals.

He points out the irony that "you can get paid lots of money to do what you don't like to do, but often to do what you love you have to risk giving up everything. I mean, the prospects of being successful as an actor are really not very encouraging. And for the kind of success that I wanted they were even bleaker, because if I did it, I wanted to be at the top."

Perhaps that is why Crash Davis plays minor leagues and Kevin Costner has made it to the majors. Costner refused to settle for any path during his "struggle" years that would not position him at the forefront of the industry in which he so badly wanted to work.

Costner admits he was well aware of the fact that to build a solid reputation as a film star, it takes time, dedication and persistence. "You want to be like Sean Connery? You want to be like Paul Newman? It's taken those guys years to do that. You can't have it that quickly. So I'm content with how my career is going. I don't consider it meteoric. I don't consider it mediocre. I'm not too proud of it, but I'm proud of it secretly," he stated. Where his own acting is concerned, Costner's feelings are similar to his feelings about baseball. He feels they are the two fields he knows best. "I *know* how to act. It's the only thing besides baseball that I understand very deeply. Everything about it – the camera, the angle, pace, motion, character – has always come naturally to me."

Before deciding on the role, Costner hit a few with director/screenwriter Ron Shelton in a batting cage. He decided to take the role due to the quality of the script, the athletic nature of the character and the now $1.5 million salary he was commanding after his smash double success in *No Way Out* and *The Untouchables*.

Costner had been struggling for years and after the success of these two films, was well on his way to becoming a leading man. Yet it was the role of Crash Davis in *Bull Durham* that seemed to win him the hearts of movie audiences.

The part was the opposite extreme of Costner's previous turn as Eliot Ness. Crash Davis was a bachelor, cocky and talkative. Eliot Ness wasn't any of these things. However, Costner did share something very important with Crash Davis – his love of fast cars. Costner, while eschewing the normal Hollywood limousine and Rolls Royce act, drives the 1968 Mustang his character did in the film. He even kept the license plate, which reads "Crash D".

Outside of work, Costner plays an occasional game of

baseball with friend and Rangers first baseman Rafael Palmeiro. Costner can be seen every so often at Arlington Stadium fielding flies and grounders and hitting a few. He wears Daugherty's uniform (number 8) and is fairly impressive at the plate.

Said batting coach Tom Robson after one game: "He was impressive, hitting from both sides of the plate against deliveries of mine." Costner modestly replied, "Ah, he was only throwing 65 miles an hour." At the end of the week Daugherty, who was batting only .176 by then, wanted to "ask him how I can get some knocks."

Following his sex scenes in *No Way Out* and *Bull Durham* ("among the hottest in cinema history," according to some reviewers), Costner was soon tagged a sex-symbol. When asked how this affects wife Cindy, he responded: "My wife's concern is what you'd probably imagine. If the situation were reversed, I don't know if I could do it. But that's the way it is, and we have to find a way to make it work. My wife says, 'We're a great team. We're a real life couple. *That's* not a love story on film; *ours* is a love story," he expressed.

Still, Costner reports that constant effort is put into the relationship in order to protect it from his on-screen involvement with his leading ladies. "It's not easy. I'm concerned about my wife and my family and how they perceive what I do. I worry about it, but I don't know what to do, because it's obvious what kind of an actor I am and that I'll be asked to play roles that are heavily involved with women. I don't look for roles like that, but I don't back down from it either. Besides, I'm more comfortable with a horse than a woman," he admitted.

Advised that his next move should be another big-budget star vehicle, Costner nevertheless chose the low-budget *Bull Durham* with first-time director Ron Shelton. The studios were none too pleased with this brash young upstart's feelings that he knew better than they did about his career. As Costner recalls, "Ron and I showed the script around town like a couple of Santa Monica hookers. Everybody was saying, 'He's going to end up without a movie again.' I knew Orion was doing another baseball film, but I took the script to them anyway. This was on a Thursday. And I said, 'You have to make a decision by noon tomorrow.' They said, 'Give us until Monday.' I said, 'No, I've run the course. I need to get on with my life.' And, I swear to God, a minute after noon on Friday, Mike Medavoy called and said O.K." A wise decision – *Bull Durham* grossed $50 million, a good deal more than Orion's other baseball film.

Comparing his career to sports is a parallel Costner loves to use when explaining the dynamics of acting. At one UCLA speaking engagement, when questioned about his leading-man/hunk image, he said, "It's like kids playing basketball. You say, 'Well, you're the big guy, you play center, and you're little and you play guard.' You look at a screenplay and you realize the kinds of things I'm going to have to do. I mean, it's painfully obvious what I should be. When I look at a script, I say, 'Well, I'm not going to play that fat guy there, it's just not going to work.' It's not my thought to go out and play the Elephant Man to prove I'm an actor. I like to think of myself as storyteller, and trying to be in the movies, trying to be seamless." Costner added, "I'd like there to be a little bit of Crash Davis in me – he had honor. He's not too good, not too bad, and if you can tap into his loyalty, I think Crash would be a very good friend.

It's important to remember that Crash's saving grace is that he can laugh at the game he loves, and at himself. And I even bought the car from the film."

Although several colleges asked Costner to play ball for them, he turned them down. Interestingly enough, Costner played almost every position as he went through high school. "What's always bothered me about sports films," he said, "is that the actors don't look as if they could really play the game."

Ron Shelton could not agree more. Having spent five years in the minor leagues and perhaps knowing well the unfulfillment the fictional Crash Davis felt, he states actor Tony Perkins' performance in the baseball film *Fear Strikes Out* represents "a low point in sports movies."

Costner and Shelton met in a bar for a few drinks after Costner signed on for the film, but before much of the other cast was selected. Shelton says "a lot of male posturing went on" and that after the drinking, Costner suggested a turn in the batting cage. The writer-director found that Costner was a capable hitter from both sides of the plate and captured some impressive switch hits by the actor in the film. After this meeting, Shelton made it a practice that other actors in the cast went through a similar "batting practice."

The film depicts Crash's attempt to ready Ebby Calvin LaLoosh (Tim Robbins) for the majors as Susan Sarandon's character offers a different type of training. As the season progresses, so does LaLoosh, but Crash and Annie find themselves at the waning ebb of their careers. As a result, they begin to drift towards each other, having little where else to drift.

Although the film ends happily, there is a certain sadness about their lives as the two begin to lean on each other. This ambivalent and touching ending is one reason Costner was so attracted to the script.

"It doesn't hinge on winning in the last game or throwing the last game, or the hero's dying in the last reel," he said. "It's about deciding what kind of person you're gonna be. Are you gonna turn alcoholic because you never made it? Are you gonna sleep with boys who are twenty-one or establish a relationship with a man who you like?" If Costner's films have a connecting thread, it's their sweetness. "The one thing that I always want to have, the reason I decided to do *Bull Durham*, is poignance. I think that whenever you can slide that into a movie you've got something. It's one thing to scare people, and it's one thing to make people laugh or give people a rush from all the actors, but it's an art form to get people in a theater and have 'em a little more on edge because there's more at stake here with these people."

Susan Sarandon shares some steamy love scenes with Costner in *Bull Durham* but says she was initially attracted to him by his love and enthusiasm for film. "Do you know that he can do every scene from *How The West Was Won*?" she recalled. "That was one of the many things that endeared me to him immediately. Anyone who can sit in your living room and act out *How The West Was Won*."

Sarandon discovered that there was more to Costner than was evident in his films. "He's paid his dues," she says. "He's had a while to figure out who he wants to be and what he's all about and what he wants to stand for. He also really understands how the industry works, so he can sit down with the power brokers and hold his own and see what games they're playing. He's very smart that way," she added.

Although for a time Costner was very uncomfortable doing sex scenes, his performance in *Durham* with Sarandon is funnier, friendlier and sexier than his encounters with Sean Young in *No Way Out*.

"I don't think anybody feels comfortable," he laments. "Number one, the actress is at a great disadvantage, because typically we show the actress more than we show the man, so there is this exploitative element, and if you like someone, you feel protective of her. I felt protective of Susan and Sean because they're in a vulnerable position, so I don't want to get lost in the acting so that something gets revealed that maybe they wouldn't want to be revealed." This protective element is what makes him also appealing to millions of women.

Sarandon appreciated that protectiveness and felt that "making *Bull Durham* with Kevin Costner was the best working experience I ever had. Kevin worries about all the right things. That's why he'll be a very good director."

There are those that say that despite his outwardly cool demeanor, Costner has quite a sense of humor. He reportedly does terrifically funny impressions of Debbie Reynolds and Karl Malden. Ron Shelton has tried to get him to consider doing a comedy since their *Bull Durham* success, but Costner has resisted so far.

As Shelton explains, "He is funny. I hope he will grow to trust that side of himself more. He's so damn good-looking and he has such a strong presence I don't know if he's been afraid to loosen up. I would grab him and do Crash at him and say, 'It's fun, God damn it – loosen up!' and he would loosen up. You're just using one part of Kevin when you cast him as the strong, silent type." Costner's seriousness apparently reflects both his desire to do a good job and his feelings of awkwardness from high school, a time when he didn't feel all that confident that he was "okay."

However, director Shelton, who was in the Baltimore Orioles farm system for a while and intimately familiar with minor league baseball, came to appreciate the fact that Costner's seriousness made "Durham" a baseball movie void of the usual Hollywood baseball movie cliches. He was especially pleased his actor was so versatile when it came to athletics.

He recalls, "He learned to call pitches, throw out base runners and block the plate (as someone named Crash would be expected to do). When he swung the bat, those were *his* line drives and home runs against darned good semi-pro pitching." Although Shelton struck out at the box office with his two other films, this one struck a homerun with the audience and producers Thom Mount and Mark Burg. *Bull Durham* was Orion's biggest financial hit for 1988, and executives looked forward to their future with Kevin Costner. No one realized that while Costner was on the way up, Orion was fast falling in the opposite direction.

The character of Crash Davis did allow Costner to loosen up a little where his screen image was concerned because he was able to play a hero that was slightly off to the left of his straight-arrow hero performances. There may be more "Crash" in Costner's own character than we all know. Costner agrees. "I think he's close to the bone because of the way he's written. This character is flawed and I'm flawed. He has a sense of humor about things, and he's sure about things."

During the filming, Costner was so into his character that one of the extras was thrown off by his realism. In one sequence, one of the bat boys has to enthusiastically tell Crash to "get a hit." Crash responds by saying, "Shut up." Costner delivered the line so firmly, however, that the young actor turned to the director, and nearly in tears, said, "Is he *supposed* to say that?"

Costner was a little more than surprised to be treated more like a veteran actor than a beginner in mid take-off. "I realized when I got with the other actors on the set they're looking to me, and I can hardly believe that... Being the lead actor to me is being a supporting actor, because you're the only one who can save a bit player," he reported.

One benefit of making *Bull Durham* (and one that has not always come his way in the business) was the friendship he made with Shelton. The eight-week shoot, which is much less time afforded the average feature, was very strenuous on the cast and crew. But Shelton came to appreciate the fact that Costner had his lines down cold and knew not only his role but the lines of everyone else as well. Costner has been known to irritate directors with numerous questions, hawk-like attention to detail and dialogue changes. Sources close to the set say there were a few argumentative exchanges between the actor and director, but Shelton confirms they were mostly "of the give-and-take variety, with a minimum collision of egos." As a result of their effort on *Durham*, Shelton and Costner say they would like to someday work together again when the right project comes their way.

The film earned Shelton an Academy Award nomination for his original script.

What the critics said about

BULL DURHAM

In THE NEW YORKER (Pauline Kael)
"Named for the chewing tobacco, the romantic comedy BULL DURHAM has the kind of dizzying off-center literacy that Preston Sturges' pictures had. It's a satirical celebration of our native jauntiness and wit; it takes us into subculture that's like a bawdy adjunct of childhood – minor-league baseball. Everybody in it is a comic character, and uses a pop lingo that you tune into without any trouble, though you can't quite believe the turns of phrase you're hearing. You're thrown just enough to do a double take, and recover in time to do another.... Kevin Costner comes through with his first wide-awake, star performance. He keeps you on his side from his very first scene.... Costner lets you see that Crash is lonely, but he underplays the loneliness; it's just a tone blended in with his other tones. He picks a fight with an umpire and goads the guy until he gets thrown off the field. (It's Costner's best scene: he's as berserkly ironic as Jack Nicholson is at some of his peaks.)"

In TIME (Richard Corliss)
"Crash Davis (Kevin Costner) is quite another species of ballplayer, the kind cursed with self-awareness.... It helps too that Ron Shelton has written the wittiest, busiest screenplay since *Moonstruck*, and that his three stars do their very best screen work. Costner's surly sexiness finally pays off here; abrading against Sarandon's earth-mam geniality and Robbins' rube egocentricity, Costner strikes sparks."

Field of Dreams

Costner decided to follow the success of *Bull Durham* with another baseball-themed film, *Field of Dreams*. As usual when Costner makes up his mind, everyone else tries to make him change it. Friends and associates have advised against nearly every film he's made since his first real success (*The Untouchables*).

As Costner laments, "I've been very lucky with stuff. But a lot of movies I end up doing no one really wants to make – I think people were laughing. Nobody wanted to make *No Way Out*, nobody wanted to make *Bull Durham*, and for the longest time nobody wanted to make *Field Of Dreams*."

These feelings were further supported by *Dreams* writer-director Phil Alden Robinson, who found out that Costner, once he makes up his mind to accomplish a goal, stands by his decision at all costs. Costner battled executives from the start who believed the film was doomed to fail because it had none of the standard elements of today's hit film: car chases, sex scenes and graphic language.

Because of the belief that the script was less than commercial, both Costner and Robinson were aware that it might be altered. Costner stood by Robinson (much as he was later to stand by the script of *Dances With Wolves* author, Michael Blake), and made sure no one tinkered with the screenplay.

Robinson recalled, "He [Costner] said to me, 'Look, you will undoubtedly feel a lot of pressure from time to time to make changes, whether it's from the studio or from yourself getting nervous. I'll be the guy standing behind you, whispering in your ear, 'Don't change a word.'"

Costner's feelings about the movie's story were strong. "Emotionally, I believed it. But it scares [movie] people when there's no sex and no violence and no action for an audience as it waits for the ace card to be played. But that ace card can be so magical, it's just like a great love courtship. It can be worth the wait."

Co-producer Charles Gordon agreed that the film takes an enormous risk. "Any class in film-writing would teach that this story contained the three elements you should never make movies about: fantasy, baseball and farming," he said.

Field of Dreams depicts the story of how Iowa farmer Ray Kinsella makes his dreams (and those of a few others) come true. True to his words to writer-director Shelton, Costner remained the motivating force throughout the picture. There were no changes made to the Shelton script before it hit the screen.

After the success of *Bull Durham*, Costner was now commanding $2.5 million per picture. The *Dreams* set was the most pleasant for Costner so far in his career. The cast included James Earl Jones, Amy Madigan and Burt Lancaster in a minor role. Cast and crew had an exceptionally pleasant experience while the film was shooting in the middle of a Dubuque cornfield, with the only difficulty being the drought-ridden Iowa summer.

However, there was some tension on the set due to a 64-day shooting schedule. As Robinson remembers, "Sixty-four times I said I'd never direct again. I had industrial-strength angst."

To reduce their stress during the filming, the crew enjoyed baseball, fishing, golf and lawn parties. Costner's family was with him on location for most of the shoot and his band Roving Boy joined him, practicing between takes and performing during cast celebrations.

Costner had begun to realize his career was taking off. He was becoming one of the "hottest" tickets in Hollywood as more and more studios clamored to get the newest leading man. Suddenly, his face was looking back at him from magazine covers. He received an invitation to the White House and became a presenter at that year's annual Academy Awards ceremony.

As all the attention grew, however, Costner realized that, along with all the rewards, he was paying a price. On the *Dreams* set, he said: "There's something in my life that's slipping away from me that I'll never have again. It's like this threatening thing that's coming to envelop me."

Also threatening to envelop Costner were every quality studio and agency in Hollywood. Before Costner began filming *Field of Dreams*, he signed with Michael Ovitz, the most powerful agent in town. His new deal reportedly had him making $3 million per picture plus a percentage of the profits.

Costner also signed a deal with Orion Studios (*No Way Out* and *Bull Durham*) which gives him the option to produce, star and/or direct. At that point in time, no one could have known that the first project Costner was going to develop, based on a Civil War soldier's diaries and tentatively entitled "Lt. Dunbar" (which would become *Dances With Wolves*), would become his biggest box-office success and win him the Academy Awards for Best Picture and Best Direction.

Dreams's baseball theme made Costner recall his youth. He began to re-experience the nagging doubts he carried with him in his youth about the direction of his life.

"I had this kind of neurosis that I think a lot of young people suffer, which is if you haven't decided what you've wanted to do by a certain age, you're a failure," he said.

Despite his previous successes – 1987's *No Way Out* and *The Untouchables* and 1988's *Bull Durham* – Costner discovered it is no easier for him to have his way where project development is concerned. But his persistence and foresight has paid off.

"Most people I trusted thought I was nuts to make *Dreams*. But they hadn't read the script. Then I started telling people what the story was about – and they *really began to think I was crazy*! When I first read *Field of Dreams*, I thought it could be my generation's 'It's A Wonderful Life,'" he said.

The movie has Costner portraying an Iowa farmer who hears a voice emanating from his cornfield which advises him to convert it to a baseball diamond. His character, Ray Kinsella, obeys and is visited by the ghost of "Shoeless" Joe Jackson and other baseball greats. Ray continues to follow the voice's instructions until he discovers what is missing in his own life.

The baseball theme is downplayed, however, causing *New Yorker* critic Pauline Kael to wonder, "Are Robinson and his producers so afraid of the supposed box-office curse on baseball movies that they don't want to risk bringing baseball into the foreground? We never get to feel for ourselves what it was that made Shoeless Joe and others love the game so much they have had to come back from the grave to play it."

Kael was not alone in her disappointment that baseball serves simply as a motif for traditional American values rather than as an integral part of the movie. *Time*'s Richard Corliss labeled it the "wussiest of male weepies." However, other reviewers found good in the film.

The movie is a metaphor for the passing of generations and for the bonding process that takes place between generations from sharing the sport of baseball. Costner has said that neither *Bull Durham* nor *Field of Dreams* is a baseball movie. "*Bull Durham* is about men and women and why they get along and why they can't get along. *Field of Dreams* is about things gone unsaid in your life. Neither one is a baseball movie," he believes. Costner feels Crash Davis and Ray Kinsella represent some of the strengths of epic Western heroes who were role models for Costner (John Wayne in *The Searchers*, Henry Fonda in *My Darling Clementine* and Jimmy Stewart in *The Man Who Shot Liberty Valance* and *How The West Was Won*).

"I think I always identified with people who show me how I want to act, what kind of man I want to be, given the limits that they're faced with. The movie idols I loved showed me what it was like to make a tough decision. It was a theatrical experience at the time, but I thought, 'I don't want to be a puss, I don't want to do the easy thing,' and when push comes to shove, what's honorable will always be honorable," he explained.

With such powerful ability to represent a role model for those young people in the audience Costner once was a part of himself, it is reassuring to hear him put so much effort into the types of roles he chooses to play. With the cinema filled with Martin Scorcese, David Lynch and Woody Allen psychos and neurotics, it is refreshing to have a leading man who strives to represent on-screen people of "strength," people who stand as a model for us to mirror in the sometimes difficult actions encountered in our own daily lives.

Perhaps this "role-model" element, in his on-screen characterizations, explains why Costner is so compared to stars of yester-year. Like the most successful box-office screen idols of the past (John Wayne, Cary Grant and even the noble females, Katharine Hepburn, Greer Garson, etc.), Costner only exhibits admirable behavior on-screen. His limitations where each character is concerned may dictate the parameters of our admiration for them, but they are all characters that strive to "do the right thing." How many audience members wish to model their behavior in reality on someone who behaves in a "psychotic" or "neurotic" manner?

This "idealized behavior" of his characters also helps to explain part of Costner's phenomenal box-office appeal. His characters and plots attract so many paying customers because we find it rare (and thus are more willing to pay for it) when people act "heroically" or "admirably," but it is quite common (and therefore not as desirable to pay for) "psychotic" or "neurotic" behavior.

For example, even though Robert DeNiro's performance as the psychotic Jake LaMotta in 1980's *Raging Bull* earned the film a Best Picture Academy Award and even though the performance won rave reviews from critics everywhere, the picture still earned less than half of the box-office gross taken in by *Bull Durham*. (*Durham* earned $22 million from U.S. and Canadian rentals – the amount the studio actually sees – while *Raging Bull* only made $10.1 million).

This was the case even though Costner's performance in the film *Bull Durham* was given only a lukewarm reception by critics. One can easily surmise that the greater appeal of *Bull Durham* is basically due to the admiration the audience possesses for Costner's character, Crash Davis, as opposed to the violent and insensitive DeNiro role. Crash represents a much more sensitive and caring human being, even if he is not as much of a career success as the heavyweight prizefighter portrayed by DeNiro.

This philosophy goes in keeping with Costner's feelings that there is a "Ten Commandments" list if you are going to be the type of matinee idol that inspires and gives strength. In his efforts to make sure the roles he plays are the kind that lend him an image similar to the screen heroes of his youth, Costner relies on the following code of behavior:

1. A man stands alone.
2. A man stands by his friends.
3. A man protects his family.
4. A man loves doing his work well.
5. A man is at home out of doors.
6. A man shares and plays fair.
7. A man speaks his mind.
8. A man hoards his smiles.
9. A man follows his dreams.
10. What a man's got is what he is.

Costner admits that he would have to go back in time to really be able to perform in the kinds of movies and roles closest to his own identity. "I'd have loved to spend five or six years in the studio system... doing all those cowboy pictures. I was born 30 years too late for the kind of cinema I'd like to do."

His *Dreams* co-stars had nothing but glowing praise and warm feelings towards Costner. James Earl Jones admires the manner in which Costner picks his roles and projects. "Kevin says he picks roles in movies where he'd like to play *all* the roles. He said he wanted to play my role in *Field of Dreams* and Amy Madigan's role, etc. I found that to be a good thing because it means that he has a healthy appreciation for other actors' jobs, not an ego attraction to the role," said Jones.

The Hollywood veteran Jones also admitted that Costner gives him a sense of deja vu concerning another screen hero – Gary Cooper. "Watching Kevin on the monitor on location, I had to admit it: it *was* Gary Cooper. For one thing, Gary Cooper was always looking to spit. He and Kevin have the same pucker in his mouth," he shared.

Says Phil Alden Robinson, "For a guy who's really fun, he's also very serious about his work. He's not just an actor who shows up and does his job." The star himself feels that at times he may take his career and acting a little too seriously. It's during those times he toys with the idea of changing courses in mid-stream. As he puts it, "I could easily live in Alaska on a river and mine gold. And trap and hunt. Very easily."

Still, those close to him say that when Costner starts talking about his alternate life courses (he also fantasizes about chucking it all to live on a farm) they turn a deaf ear. His friend and former director Kevin Reynolds laughs at this notion of Costner being contented so easily. "Maybe for a while," he suggests, "but it would drive him crazy sooner or later."

Costner chalks up all the success for *Dreams* to Robinson, but he does like to admit when he's improvised something that works well. He recalls several such contributions. "When Ray is throwing to Shoeless Joe, he gets so excited that he glances back to the house to see if his wife is looking. When Ray is walking toward his dad, picking at his hand, and, realizing that his dad is doing the same thing, he quickly puts his hands down. And his run to the mound isn't a completely athletic run. It's a little funny. There's some English on it. Those things are mine and nobody else's."

Costner's one regret is that the film's running time is not longer. He explains its length by saying, "I guess they felt people would get restless and say, 'Hey, Kev's not throwing a *rake* at anybody, he's certainly not *fucking*, so what do we got here, a Care Bear movie?'" The script may not have impressed executives, but it was a good enough story to garner Phil Alden Robinson an Oscar nomination for Best Screenplay Adaptation.

Costner admits that the story was hard to pull off due to its fantasy elements (ghosts) and its sentimentality (the father of Ray appears along with the other ghosts). Canadian author W.P. Kinsella, whose 1982 novel *Shoeless Joe* was the basis for *Dreams*, appreciated Costner's attraction to his story. He told *Maclean's*: "Costner has a tremendous presence about him. He engages you with his eyes. Whether he's in front of the camera or not, he can control any scene that he's in without realizing it. It's not something that he has worked at – he seems to have been born with it."

Costner's attraction to the role is based in part on the fact that it reminded him of his own relationship with his father. It also held the additional attraction of Burt Lancaster in a minor role. Costner confesses to nothing but respect for the man and his career. He does admit, though, that he hopes his children see him more as a "Spencer Tracy" type, because that's the way he viewed his own father.

On being a role model onscreen and off, Costner comments, "You have to try to conduct your life in some way and if you don't know how to do that and you haven't heard the voice in the cornfield, then you look for images and patterns. Movie heroes are great patterns. For me, a film idol is anyone who's ever done the right thing in a situation where I wasn't sure what I would have done."

However, the film's theme of unresolved differences between parent and child caused Costner to reflect on his father's unsupportive feelings towards him when he was a struggling actor and his refusal to follow his father's advice to take a conventional job for security. Costner felt particularly vulnerable because he received financial assistance from his father from time to time.

"*Field of Dreams* is about things gone undone in your life. There was a period in my life when my dad didn't think I was a very responsible person. And I thought I was. I had left the house but still would need things from him. You'd get in trouble, you'd need stuff. And it was like he could have told you that was going to happen," the younger Costner recalled.

This lack of parental faith in his career was what actually made Costner more determined to succeed. Since he has succeeded, he has come full-circle and enjoys a positive relationship with his father, often inviting his parents to join him on location.

What the critics said about

FIELD OF DREAMS

In THE NEW YORKER (Pauline Kael)
"*Field of Dreams* is a crock – a kinder, gentler crock.... Amy Madigan does quick, amused line readings, and in the early

scenes she and Costner spark each other... and though for the rest of the movie he's playing an earnest, visionary boob, he does it with conviction. He's James Stewart (who is seen in 'Harvey' on the farmhouse TV) and Gary Cooper in their Frank Capra roles; this is the kind of American-hero acting in which only good thoughts enter the hero's mind and moonlight bounces off his teeth."

In TIME (Richard Corliss)

"The hero of Phil Alden Robinson's *Field of Dreams* is a farmer (Kevin Costner) who dreams of bringing Shoeless Joe Jackson back to earth for one more game.... Despite a lovely cameo turn by Burt Lancaster, *Field of Dreams* is the male weepie at its wussiest."

In THE NEW REPUBLIC (Stanley Kauffmann)

"Phil Alden Robinson, the director, wrote the screenplay from a novel by W.P. Kinsella. The first few minutes with voice-over by Kevin Costner, who plays the lead, create some goodwill toward the film, but very soon it's betrayed as the screenplay lurches wildly."

CHAPTER

6

DANCES WITH WOLVES

The making of *Dances With Wolves* represents a turning point in the career and character of Kevin Costner. As he himself admitted about the making of the film, "Directing *Dances With Wolves* was the most difficult thing I've done in my life. I've probably learned more things about myself from this than from any other experience. I can't tell you what those things are – they're kind of private and they're my own personal scorecard. But I didn't know if I could handle the situation, and the bottom line is I did handle it."

Dances With Wolves was a family affair for the Costners in the sense that Kevin's parents, wife Cindy and three children all appeared in the film in minor roles. Charges of nepotism were leveled at Costner for putting his entire family into the film, but as he replied, "I know people wonder why I gave those roles to my family. Well, I just did it and I can't explain why. I never want to be a stranger to my kids, so I make them very much a part of my world." You will have to be quite observant to catch the Costner family while viewing *Dances With Wolves* on video cassette or cable TV – they are all wiped out in one massacre scene. However, illustrating how close the Costners really are, his mother and father parked their travel trailer at the Dakota location and even installed a phone.

Costner is a family-oriented individual and leaned on them during the difficult production of *Dances With Wolves*. When asked about the conflict of work and family, Costner answered in his typically honest way, "It's weird. You sometimes find yourself thinking, 'I could do this better if I was by myself.' Then you think, 'Yet I'd miss two months with my son – two months with my family.' So the price you pay for not being alone is there. But there's this other thing, experiencing your family, that you can *never* put a price on."

Dances With Wolves is a perfect example of the auteur dream realized. Kevin Costner stood behind his vision of the film from the time of its conception to the time of its release nearly two and a half years later. *Dances* was born one evening as Kevin sat with Jim Wilson and *Dances* author and screenwriter Michael Blake in his living room. Wilson met Blake in film school at Berkeley, and the pair collaborated on *Stacy's Knights*, a low-budget gambling picture set in Reno in which Costner played the lead role of Will Bonner. The film marked the first time Wilson was paid to direct and Blake was paid to write a screenplay. Costner was also given his first real break – the lead – as a result.

Stacy's Knights was a failure and it would be another eight years before the three would be reunited on a film set. It was in 1986 that Michael Blake voiced his frustrations over having none of his screenplays optioned to his friend Kevin Costner. "Write a novel. If you write a script, it will just end up there," Costner replied, pointing to a stack of twenty scripts sitting in the corner. The writer had little to lose and during the next year, while friends Jim Wilson and Kevin Costner fed and housed him, Blake wrote a story about Lt. John J. Dunbar and his experiences among the Sioux.

While Costner and Wilson thought there was a great film in the story, they made no commitments to Blake, who moved back to Arizona when the book was finished and resumed his dishwashing career. Almost immediately, says Blake, "I received a call from Kevin telling me to start writing the screenplay. He was involved every step of the way."

The three friends and co-workers spent the next two and a half years on a draft that, six versions later, finally satisfied Costner. Nelson Entertainment and Island Pictures were the first two film companies to whom Tig Production partners Wilson and Costner offered the script. It sat around for over a year at Nelson Entertainment and for six months at Island Pictures.

After one financing frustration after another, Costner and Wilson decided to raise the films production money on their own. They sold the foreign rights to the film first and were able to raise nearly 40% of the required capital. They started pre-production with this amount and signed a deal with Orion two weeks before shooting commenced that gave them the necessary amount to finish the film. The deal also gave control of final cut on the film to Costner, a rare privilege for first-time directors.

The final film, for all intents and purposes, is the vision Kevin Costner wanted on the screen, not studio executives. However, there is a four-hour version of *Dances With Wolves* that is being prepared for release sometime in the future. There are more courtship scenes between Lt. Dunbar and Stands With A Fist, and an explanation of what happened at the abandoned garrison outpost before Lt. Dunbar first arrives there. The same level of dedication and perfection that went into making the film will accompany the release of any longer version.

According to Jim Wilson, "There are still months of work to be done and it's premature" to speculate about the expanded version. "It may go straight to television as a two- or three-part miniseries or it may be released theatrically." A video of the longer version would then be released. The longer version may be put together with a half-hour documentary on the making of *Dances With Wolves* as a special package. A theatrical release of the longer version will more than likely be limited to select cities.

Concerning his subject matter, even Costner agrees it goes against Hollywood tradition. "It's a dumb first movie... full of kids, animals, first-time actors speaking in a foreign language. A period piece on top of that. But I'm just offering up the film, letting the people decide." Subtitles were used frequently throughout the film for the Lakota Sioux dialogue.

The picture's subject also goes directly against the widely-accepted Hollywood belief that the Western is a dead genre. In fact, the film review in "Variety" warmly received the film and underlined the fact that "it's clear the filmmakers were proceeding without regard for the rules. Their audacity in doing so, because they knew what they had, is as inspiring as the film itself."

Costner, noted for being a perfectionist, tried to avert disaster and plan for his final vision every step of the way. *Dance With Wolves* was shot mostly in the outback of South Dakota. The filming ran a month over its originally anticipated shooting schedule to make a film that is epic in scope. There are parts for over 150 Civil War soldiers and just more than 175 Sioux. The total cast numbers close to 500 with 48 speaking roles. The crew numbered more than 130 and there were 3,500 buffalo, 42 wagons and the more than 300 horses.

Temperatures in the summer ran as high as 115 degrees and there were days when the mercury barely hit 20 degrees once fall arrived. To get as many Native Americans as they needed, the producers took advertisements out in the Lakota Times and held auditions throughout America and in Canada. In addition, a Sioux village with 45 lodges had to be built in South Dakota.

There were plenty of other problems in creating the look, feel and mood Costner wanted in the three-hour story told through four seasons. The action was to occur in the fall for some scenes, but it was logistically impossible to shoot some of them in the fall.

As a result, the season was literally painted in by using more than 10,000 gallons of paint to give the leaves on the trees a look that was Eastern autumn. Similar to the red earth of Tara not being red enough for David O. Selznick during the making of *Gone With The Wind*, so the grass of South Dakota was too brown for Kevin Costner and he had Jeffrey Beecroft, the production designer, supervise the process of dying it green.

Accents were also a major problem for the cast, including the Native Americans. Omaha tribesman Rodney Grant plays Wind In His Hair in *Dances With Wolves*. He gives an alive performance filled with great spirit and dignity. However, in rehearsals he caused a few people to lose their tempers over his accent difficulties. Costner had a month slated for language rehearsals but Grant was so hopeless that Costner made him go back for more. "I don't want another rehearsal until you get the lines down," Costner snapped.

At this point Elisabeth Leustig, the casting director who helped Costner select Grant, started to drill Grant. He finally got fed up with her bullying ("My ass was on the line," she later stated) and said "Enough." Leustig is an easygoing woman but her temper finally surfaced. "I don't have to do this," she told Grant, who was well aware that he could be demoted to a bit part.

Grant stalked off the set and sulked for a while before returning to Leustig and apologizing. "I'm sorry. I'm gonna make you proud of me," he told her. A few hours later, Grant was being congratulated by Costner on his performance in the scene where he first challenges Lt. Dunbar: "That was beautiful, Rodney. That was magic."

Costner himself had help learning the language from Doris Leader Charge, a teacher of the Lakota Sioux language who plays the chief's wife in *Dances With Wolves*.

Perhaps one of the most dangerous incidents that occurred on the set of *Dances With Wolves* was due to Costner's passion for doing many of his own stunts. He did quite a few of the stunts in *The Untouchables* and *No Way Out*. Due to this reputation, Costner is considered a bad insurance risk. Costner's character had to ride through a herd of 3,500 stampeeding buffaloes while pretending to shoot. Costner and many of the Indians also had to learn to ride bareback.

The buffalo were procured from nearby privately owned herds (a main reason the producers chose this area). Producer Wilson and stunt coordinator Jim Howell tried to talk their star out of it, but to no avail. Even Cindy Costner tried to stop him from doing the dangerous shot, but her efforts were in vain also. "I was really nervous. I was making myself physically ill. I couldn't tell him what to do when he was directing *Dances*. At night I could chew on him a little bit, but he was gonna go out there the next day and do what he wanted to do," she recalled.

A certain spirit took hold of Costner while filming the buffalo hunt. "The buffalo were snorting and mad as hell – they're the most incredible beasts when they're terrified. I'd never experienced anything like it, nor had the 20 Indian riders that I'd asked to ride in among the herd. There was a great amount of fear the first day we did it, but after that it gave a chance for those particular riders to connect with something very deep inside them. One of them said to me, 'You know, I felt a horn brush my leg,' and I knew what he was talking about because I was in the middle of it, too. While this is an experience everyone else can enjoy cinematically, it gave us a kind of personal fraternity because we were out there enacting, at full flight, something that hasn't happened for a hundred years," Costner explained.

Co-star Mary McDonnell was also awed by the event. "The spiritual life of the Sioux emerged in a very subtle and unordained way. When it occurred you could feel around you a kind of genetic understanding of the importance of that moment for the tribe. It was a moment that appealed to something higher, and to the awareness of its loss at the same time. I found that both very sad and uplifting."

Michael Blake will never forget the exciting but terrifying incident. "Kevin took one of the most hellacious falls I've ever seen in my life. I'm going to get it on tape, because it's one of the worst falls from a horse you'll ever see. Here's what happened: Kevin's horse is going along straight, then the Indian rider comes sideways and loses control of his horse, just like a car accident. Bam! Kevin goes straight up in the air, somehow twists and is coming down facing backwards while his horse is at full speed. Kevin hits the ground, bounces about two feet straight up in the air and rolls over like a big sack of flour," he remembers with a shudder.

Perhaps most remarkably, the accident only momentarily shook the dazed Costner. Upon returning to his feet, he tucked his army pants into his boots, remounted, and told Norman Howell, "I want to ride." One appreciates Costner's courage but also the concerns of nervous insurance investors.

The film began to take its toll on the novice director towards completion of filming, and in unguarded moments, Costner would admit, "I don't know why I set myself up for such scrutiny. In the privacy of my room, I'll wonder if I've bitten off too much and whether I'll make it. There's a nauseousness that goes along with it. I have to answer for all this."

Costner was so stressed during the production that he lost fifteen pounds and added crow's feet to his face and weariness to his character. "Orion officials secretly worried [about the film's three-hour plus original length]. It's almost as if I knew what they were gonna say before they said it: 'First-time fucking director doesn't know how to cut his film.' Had I had *complete* brass fucking balls and not given a shit what anybody thought, it would have been about three hours [and] fifteen [minutes]," he said.

Mary McDonnell was chosen, according to Costner, because she was a "real woman." He had seen thousands of actresses, but Mary was his idea of someone who had not only beauty but experience, warmth and understanding built into her features.

Although McDonnell enjoyed the overall process of making *Dances With Wolves*, she discovered that the myth about Kevin Costner being "laid back" was unfounded. "He's a very complicated man, but in a wonderful way. There's nothing laid back about him at all. As much as there's an easygoing personality there, he's very focused, almost obsessed. Underneath all that warm personality is a driven workhorse," she recalled.

Co-producer Jim Wilson says of the film's direction: "It [the film] ran over for the simple reason that we were trying to make the best movie we could – you could call it 'added showmanship.' Come hell or highwater, we were going to see that it got done properly, so I never held up a clock to his face and said, 'Kevin, the time is ticking away.' He damn well knew it was. I can't say he wasn't prepared, although he's not what you'd call methodical as a director. We stuck to the script, more or less, but many of his ideas came out then and there, and that's just how the picture was made."

Out of fear of offending Costner, Orion finally agreed to give him control of the film, but still handled its distribution. A completion-bond company was hired to report on the film, however, and soon into production it was realized Costner would go over schedule and over budget. Jim Wilson held an early morning meeting with Costner, who agreed to put up part of his $5 million salary as a guarantee against escalating costs.

In the end, the film was only five percent over its projected cost of $18 million and Costner had contributed $2.9 million of his salary to cover the costs of his expanded shooting schedule. When the film's financial troubles became known, the picture was immediately dubbed "Kevin's Gate" by Hollywood wags, a reference to the film whose title has come to symbolize big-budget, egomaniacal failure in Hollywood, Michael Cimino's *Heaven's Gate*.

Costner bristles at that allusion and defends the film as a "bargain" for $18 million. He insists no studio could have put as much substance on film as he has for so little cost.

Costner had the final laugh when the approximately $21 million film grossed more than $164 million in the U.S. and Canada alone. Still, he harbors much resentment against the bond company that kept the pressure on him.

"I offered to buy them out a week into the movie. I told

them, 'I'll pay your salary, just get the fuck out of my life.' That shocked the shit out of them. They are necessary for people who do runaway things. But to people who are fiscally responsible, they're a giant pain in the ass. They endanger a project that's trying to run the line. They start telling you you can't do things. I ended up doing everything I wanted."

Outside of meddling with his "baby," Costner had sympathetic words for the cash-ailing Orion Pictures. "They're experiencing a cycle that's not pleasant by anyone's standards, but if you go back beyond this award, you'll see that Orion has made a lot of good choices in the past," he said after his Oscar victory.

These comments, though generous, hardly reflect Orion's track record. Richard Sean Lyon points out in his *Survival Guide To Film* (LyonHeart publishers) that Orion's batting average is so low that "Crash Davis" (Costner's *Bull Durham* character) would be throughly ashamed.

In 1987, the company only made three films out of fifteen that returned their costs from their U.S. and Canadian distribution. This 20% average was reduced in 1988 to 18%, when, out of 17 features produced, only three returned their cost once more.

Finally, in 1989, Orion dropped to a seven percent average by having only one film, *Dances With Wolves*, return its cost from U.S. and Canadian distribution. Without Costner's films, it's likely the troubled Orion would have been in financial straits even sooner.

Costner has remained aloof from the criticism leveled at *Dances With Wolves* regarding its naive historical outlook and against-the-rules ingredients. "My only concern is whether the movie is good. And I think it is. I have no control after that. My friends are afraid I'm going to be eaten up. They know I've put my heart in it, up there on the block for anyone to do with it what they will. But I don't care what Hollywood thinks. You can underline that," he said.

After winning seven out of twelve Academy Awards on the night of March 25, 1991, all of Costner's risks and instincts seemed proven correct. Costner picked up the Academy statues for Best Direction and Best Picture (along with Jim Wilson) from Barbra Streisand, who could not have been more aware that first-time directors seldom garner such lofty acclaim. Her first credited attempt at directing, 1983's *Yentl*, was not nominated by the Academy in any major category, though Streisand did win the Golden Globe for Best Direction.

Dances With Wolves had been considered a favorite at Oscar time; in fact there was much talk of an anticipated "sweep." Costner had already won the Director's Guild of America Award and the Golden Globe for directing and producing.

Costner thanked his friends Jim Wilson and Micahel Blake, saying, "Everyone knows you don't make pictures yourself." After such a sweeping victory, he was even generous to the film's financiers, Executive Producer Jake Eberts and Majestic Films International's Guy East, "who figured out through all my boyish enthusiasm that I was deadly serious making this movie."

Orion executives even came in for some praise themselves, as did Michael Ovitz, head of Creative Artists Agency and generally considered the most powerful deal-maker in Hollywood. Costner thanked him for "helping me finish *Dances* without compromising any of my dreams."

Critics were disappointed by Costner's "aw-shucks"

acceptance speech and reference to how "the people he went to school with will remember this." One report characterized him as an "arrogant Sally Field." The *Village Voice* agreed: "The moment you referred to your own boyish enthusiasm was the moment 100 million women fell into severe depression because the fantasies they'd been nurturing for years were shattered into bits! Oh why, Kevin, why?"

Critics also picked up on this softness, both in Costner and the fictional Lt. Dunbar. "John J. Dunbar is an almost too perfect example of the new American male, that improbable beau ideal who has been created out of recent feminist fantasies and the failure of certain old-fashioned masculine dreams," wrote critic Richard Schickel.

Schickel hits upon a major point when he says Costner appeals to feminist fantasies. If *Gone With The Wind* were being cast today, Costner would have to play Ashley. He's too soft, too much of a "gentleman" to play someone like Rhett, who must resort to all types of behavior to survive against a world torn by war.

Costner has stated *Dances* is his "love letter to the past," similarly to Ashley, who could not forget about his love of the "gone forever" past. Like his character Elliot Ness in *The Untouchables*, Costner would only be prepared to do anything he could "within the law," much as Ashley only exhibited behavior that was "proper."

This is why the Costner image is only a fantasy of what women want, not a reality. What is "proper" is not always what is "best." Women may say they want this quality in a hero, but the screen heroes who have had the most indelible and strongest images over time with audiences are the ones who went outside of the "law" when justice and integrity demanded it: Bogart, Gable and Wayne.

It was Cary Grant, Gary Cooper and Jimmy Stewart who, like Costner, had to be provoked before doing anything "improper." Women may prefer that softness at home, but when their hero is out in the real world fighting for their survival, they choose the hero who sometimes goes beyond what is considered "proper" behavior. A "proper" dead husband may be more noble, but much less practical than a socially ostracized live one.

This softer side of Costner's characters was also analyzed by noted journalist Barbara Lippert. "Certainly Lt. Dunbar, a.k.a. D.W.Wolves, is a kind of new-age hero – half John Wayne, half Shirley Maclaine. The spiritual is often seen as feminine. Perhaps it's also this oddball combination of buffalo-stomping masculinity and soft spirituality that women find so appealing. Costner's feminized sexual manifesto is expressed in several of his screen roles."

Still, it is hard to imagine "The Duke" in *Bull Durham* as Crash Davis wearing Annie's flowered kimono and painting her toenails. Jimmy Stewart? Gary Cooper? Perhaps. Never Gable, Bogart or Wayne.

The films of Costner are a fantasy of how life should be if the world were perfect. The films of Gable, Bogart and Wayne showed them finding justice and some peace of mind in an imperfect system. The Grant, Cooper, Stewart and Costner films make us long for a perfect system. Both groups of actors were reponsible for many entertaining "escapist" films.

However, their characters seem to have this distinction in the roles they chose to play. Even Costner admits his screen characters are idealized and would never be permitted to exist in reality. "The honorable man is an easy target. But I don't want to pretend that I am as brave as the characters I've played. The politicians look on an honorable man and say, 'We can fuck him eight ways to Sunday. We know how to do it. We can make this honorable man look like a fucking fool.' The movies represent what happens when the hero acts in the heat of dilemma, and that's really what films are all about for me: dilemma. You're not sure what the hero will do. We like to think that he will do the right thing – in movies. We don't necessarily admire it in our own world, because we know it's political suicide," he says.

It is disheartening to find so little hope or enthusiasm for society in a celebrity with such a significant voice. Gable, Wayne, Bogart and even Cooper, Stewart and Grant did not give a damn about the mechanics of "politics." They did exactly what Costner says he does on screen – the right thing in a dilemma.

However, to say this is impossible to do in real life is to say we should not strive for morals and values off-screen (i.e., sometimes choose *not* to do the right thing) that might hold one back socially and politically. An individual responsible for being a role model for so many should consider the fact that he needs an on-screen philosophy that is practical in the real world if he expects us to adopts his on-screen values and examples in real life.

In other words, maybe the characters of Kevin Costner need to become less "kinder" and "gentler." Nonetheless, his comments about wanting to be admired politically are frightening – especially considering his liberal on-screen image but his off-screen contributions to right-wing politicians.

It seems Costner wants to be admired more than he wants to serve justice and integrity. To do the latter one must often offend the very people who represent the opportunities for our material gain.

Although Costner brings roles to the screen of heroes in the vein of Jimmy Stewart's Mr. Smith, he does not necessarily believe in them. "When we watch a movie we say, 'God bless this man, that he can be this voice.' In real life, Mr. Smith would never have gone to Washington. He would have been made to look like the village idiot. He would have been locked up. It would be made out that he hadn't paid his taxes and had eight affairs. He would be done. And he would be the same man. Integrity is out of fashion. Maybe that's why we respond to it in films," Costner said in reponse to his beliefs about screen heroes.

However, Costner's lack of historical perspective is shown by his remark that integrity is out of fashion. Reading Will and Ariel Durant's *History Of The World*, covering 3,600 years of recorded history, should make him a firm believer that integrity has never been "in fashion" in "some" circles. Still, this has not stopped countless men from being brave and courageous and going against the system to make the world a better place. To say they could not succeed is to ignore the contribution to society by men like John F. Kennedy, Ghandi and Martin Luther King just because cowards shortened the duration of their life.

This is not to say Kevin Costner and his New Age following do not want a "kinder," "gentler" world, but in the words of Thomas Jefferson, "The tree of liberty must be refreshed from time to time with the blood of patriots and tyrants. It is its natural manure." Freedom of the kind where it is safe to be unpopular has never existed. The dangers and risks associated with being "out of fashion," but correct, are elements with which any would-be or existing hero must deal.

Also recognized for their work in *Dances* were Dean Semler and Neil Travis, who received Academy Awards for beautiful cinematography and editing work, respectively. Aware of his lack of technical expertise as a first-time director, Costner explained, "I'm a more-is-better type of director. If something is good, I don't want it to end. All the camera work in the world can't disguise the lack of story. We've become factories, giving up the idea that good stories are good for us. I try to keep things as intimate as possible instead of dazzling people with my camera work. Anyhow, technical skill is something I don't possess... so I'd get caught."

In fact, Costner's long-time friend and director Kevin Reynolds came onto the set to do some shooting himself. There were rumors this was due to Orion executive worries about their first-time director, as well as Costner's belief that his own efforts could be bolstered by Reynolds' experience and advice.

Oscar-winning editor Neil Travis feels that sole credit belongs to Costner. He says Reynolds "showed up on the *Wolves* location for two weeks second-unit filming things like wagons crossing the plains, but he never once directed an actor or plotted out a scene. That was solely Kevin, and Kevin was amazingly brilliant, as far as I'm concerned." The truth is Reynolds did shoot some footage and inserts, but Costner had the whole film storyboarded in advance and directed the majority of the film.

One interesting irony connected to the movie is NBC's failure to pick up on the Little Big Horn drama *Son Of The Morning Star* while Costner was still attached to it. Costner wanted the role of General Custer after completing work on *Silverado*. According to *Son* executive producer Preston

Fischer, however, "NBC didn't think Costner was a big enough star."

Son, like *Dances*, featured Native Americans speaking in their own language. With the enormous success of *Dances*, NBC executives pushed *Son* by airing it during the enormous popularity of *Wolves*.

One more executive in Hollywood had to bemoan his lack of commercial foresight, but, as *Hunt For Red October* Producer Mace Neufeld says, "I don't think anyone in Hollywood could have predicted the success of *Dances With Wolves*."

One of Michael Blake's major sources of inspiration for writing *Dances With Wolves* was his emotional reaction while reading Dee Brown's *Bury My Heart At Wounded Knee*. However, it has been revealed over the past few years that Brown's book is selective in its recreation of that event. It has been labeled "pro-Indian" for just that reason. Regardless of that fact, there is no one who missed the point that, in spite of its huge commercial success, *Dances With Wolves* is one of the most anachronistic films ever made.

Dances With Wolves was the first Western to win Best Picture since 1931's *Cimarron* some sixty years earlier. The seven Academy Awards afforded to *Dances With Wolves* also holds the all-time record for Oscars won by a Western.

By winning the directing Oscar on his first try, Costner is only the fifth person to do so. He joins the company of Delbert Mann (1955's *Marty*), Jerome Robbins (1961's *West Side Story* – codirected by Robert Wise), Robert Redford (1980's *Ordinary People*), and James L. Brooks (1983's *Terms Of Endearment*).

On winning the award, Costner said, "I didn't think I'd win. I wasn't a big achiever in high school and I'm not particularly used to winning." When asked if he feels any pressure to follow up his success of *Wolves*, he said, "I'm not panicked about my next choice. If *Dances* is to become the movie of my career, if it reminds people of me, I won't run from its shadow."

Despite his huge victory, Costner does not believe March 25 was the greatest night of his life. "My life is bigger than the movies and my ideas are bigger than the movies. But it remains a great moment for me that no one can take away."

It is hard for many Hollywood insiders to imagine someone thinking their non-career life and ideas are bigger than a professional life that is spent "making millions happy" by creating a movie that is significant enough to attract over $200 million worth of ticket-holders into theaters in Canada and the U.S. alone. Apparently Costner, like many performers, deflates the significance of his career achievements in order to cast the spotlight away from his already attention-getting activites and to refocus it so that his family remains a significant aspect of his life.

With such a successful public career, both Costners admit this is hard to do. Any praise or criticism that is heard around the Costner house usually centers on Kevin. Cindy must be strong in order to handle that as well as the tempestuous on-screen love scenes Costner has played during the course of his film career.

During the Academy ceremony Costner also thanked his "Native American brothers and sisters, especially the Lakota Sioux, who, like himself and his family, will never forget the honor." Canadian Oneida Indian actor Graham Greene was also nominated for the Supporting Actor Oscar.

Michael Blake picked up the Academy Award for Best

Screenplay Adaptation from his own work. He took Native American *Dances With Wolves* cast member Doris Leader Charge on stage with him in order to interpret his acceptance speech in the Lakota language.

Blake also received the Writer's Guild Of America award for his screenplay, and, in his Oscar acceptance speech he stated, "The dream came to me to do something beneficial for as many people as I could. The miracle of *Dances With Wolves* proves that this kind of dream can come true."

He continued by paying homage to "the Native American nation throughout this wonderful country whose drum continues to beat and will beat forever." Even Costner admitted the credit for *Dances With Wolves* was Michael Blake's. "I'm not in the message business. The story reflects what Michael wrote. It's not my invention. I agreed with the sentiment of the movie, not the politics."

Costner's still-bitter feelings towards the Hollywood executives he clashed with during the filming of *Dances* was evident in the speech he gave at the Independent Spirit Awards later that month. Costner was the keynote speaker and more than a few chins had to be scraped off the floor when he stated that movies are hurried into theaters before properly completed, ending up as an "incomplete, half thought-out piece of shit."

Costner also voiced his optimism that by making so many mistakes, studios only increase the number of opportunities for independent filmmakers. However, he warned would-be filmmakers not to "Rationalize your projects on a fast track to destruction by saying, 'What the hell? This piece is as good as the shit that's playing in the theaters.' "

These rather bold statements made one industry insider comment, "Who made him God?" However, Costner replied that he controls his ego after the enormous success of *Dances With Wolves* by "keeping myself in check simply because it still matters to me what people like my parents and friends think of me. And that's a very good way to guide yourself."

Regardless of the shock waves sent by Costner that evening, co-producer Jim Wilson offended many with his comment that "out of sheer necessity... 'Wilstein' became my last [name]."

Supporters of Wilson within Tig Productions insisted it was just a harmless "White Anglo-Saxon's joke about learning to squeeze a buck," but many movie industry individuals did not find it so funny. "It perpetuates a gross, insensitive stereotype," complained one. The incident led one New York periodical to run a story entitled, "'DANCES' MEN: WOLVES IN CREEPS' CLOTHING?"

One of the native Canadian actors in *Dances With Wolves* Tantoo Cardinal, says making the film reminded her of a prediction by a native chief whose people were in jeopardy due to the Canadian Prairies railroads. "He said, 'The white men are blinded and deafened by greed, but there will be a generation of their children who will be our friends,'" she recalled.

Costner feels the making of *Dances With Wolves* was also an acceptance about the murkier side of American politics and genocide.

"It's a chapter we know so well, but nobody wants to put the label *genocide* on it. We won't acknowledge how many Indian cultures we destroyed. But that's our Brazilian rain forest, right there. When you look at this part of the country, you realize there was a lot of bloodshed over ownership of the land, like we had to have this. But if you fly over this land now, nobody's here, not really. There's Denver and Kansas City, and Rapid City over here. But the reality is – we didn't have to have it," he said.

Costner's Southern California upbringing shows here when he expresses 'nobody's here, not really.' He seemingly writes off the necessity of land owned by states and millions of people because they do not number the high-density populations of Los Angeles or Denver.

In addition, what about the political injustices done to the Mexican inhabitants of California during the Mexican-American War? Is Los Angeles unecessary because of injustices done to the Mexican culture during this period? High technology urban centers like Los Angeles, Kansas City and Denver now exist with all the by-products of technological development.

It is hard to imagine a people living in between them that were so unsophisticated they had no knowledge of writing, metal or the wheel.

Despite the validity of Costner's statement, the Dakota Sioux were also far from the idealized "war-only-for-survival" image Costner has presented them as exhibiting in *Dances With Wolves*. In an essay in the March 1991, "Commentary," Richard Grenier offers evidence that the Dakota Sioux tribes were brutal, aggressive and merciless:

"In the middle of the Civil War, 1862, the year of Antietam, the Sioux, threatened by the ever westward movement of the frontier, exploded in what historians Robert M. Utley and Wilcomb Washburn call 'one of the most savage and bloody Indian uprisings in history.' On the first day alone, a 'nightmare of fire and death' took the lives of 400 settlers.

"The Sioux swept through the Redwood Agency in Minnesota, massacring the men, burning the buildings, and carrying the women and children off into captivity. No one was spared. In a week, almost 1,000 white settlers had died at the hands of the Sioux."

"'In wide-ranging parties they spread over the countryside, killing, raping, pillaging and burning.' Also torturing. Some 30,000 frontier settlers fled to the East, and the outbreak kept the entire Great Plains in turmoil for fully eight years."

Even if there had been no major confrontation in 1862, the Great Plains tribes generally considered any stranger who appeared in their midst as a trespasser and a threat, to be killed immediately if possible. Clark Wissler, the late curator of the department of anthropology at the American Museum of Natural History, also affirms this aggressiveness.

As Greneir says in his essay, "'One thing is certain, the whites did not bring war to the Dakota [Sioux]. For centuries they had been schooled in arms. Their raids were never against other Dakota tribes, but that was the limit of their friendliness, for not even other members of their Siouan family were safe.'"

In *Pawnee Passage*, Martha Royce Blaine, wife of Pawnee Head Chief Garland J. Blaine, states that "The fiercest and most predatory Sioux bands were the Brule and Oglala." Blaine theorizes that the enormous number of Pawnee women murdered by the Sioux because of their value as economic and population providers is one good motive for the Pawnee resorting to such atypical behavior as helpng the white man by serving as guides. One thing is certain, the Sioux were more fierce and complex than the dreamy image of them portrayed in *Dances With Wolves*.

Digging deeper than an idealized image as the reason behind *Dances With Wolves'* enormous box-office success, one does gain added insight into the cultural values we can adopt from these primitive cultures. As an $80,000 full-page ad in the New York Times (seeking funding for the erection of a National Museum for Native Americans) read:

"...Their insight into the delicate balance between man and nature offers us a timely environmental message. Their ethic of 'sharing' provides an inspirational model for today's society. Their systems of governance paralleled many of the concepts our forefathers used to frame the Constitution. And their view of the universe and insights into astronomy may well help us chart our future in space."

One can see that the modern-day audiences that have chosen this film as a message of New Age environmentalism, and as a kinder, gentler portrayal of Native Americans, are as unaware of actual history as is Costner. Of course, Costner has said he was not out to "set history straight," but one can see that his image of the Sioux Indians is an heroic and idealized one. Costner has given us universal images of the Sioux as a loving, generous, emotional people – images too seldom seen in the Indian characters of countless Westerns before *Dances With Wolves* – but it is unlikely anyone has gained a more intellectual knowledge of American history from this film.

Ironically, one of the most authentic examples of Native American culture is flawed by its otherwise perfectionist director's lack of explanation. When Stands With A Fist is first encountered by Lt. Dunbar she is soaked in blood, but we are never told why. Although we later discover she is in mourning, but it is never explained that wives of Oglala warriors gashed their legs as a sign of grief.

No one seemed as appreciative of Costner's efforts as did different Native cultures, who thanked him by letters, awards and acceptance. In response to this, Costner said, "I haven't heard anything negative [from tham about the film], but I'm sure that in some corners there have been problems. Generally, it has been a real awakening. I have gotten letters from Native Americans in the business world, who have written to say, 'I had forgotten who I was.' Some of them are very, very emotional – the type of letters where you can actually see sentences stop on the page... You can see the writers trying to collect themselves."

Costner feels his portrayal of Indians in *Dances With Wolves* will make it quite hard for any filmmaker to revert to the old stereotyped film images of them. In this sense, Costner has shown us a different perspective than we normally are given concerning Native Americans. Although audiences may have been manipulated to the other extreme in *Dances*, it is a logical physical reaction before balance can occur, when the pendulum of prejudice was so far to the other extreme for so many years.

As the director admits about his portrayal, he was not rewriting or setting history straight, but "what I tried to show were the Indians interacting with each other, and within those interactions I put them into situations that are universally recognizable. I showed them speaking, I showed them with a thought process, and I showed them confronting their problems – which in certain instances means that they are confused and don't always know what to do. That seemed to me to be different from the way the Indians had been portrayed in the past. I show them the way I always felt about them. From the age of seven, I knew they were not monsters or comedic or lacking in dignity. I knew them to be a formidable people, as some movies, like *The Searchers*, portrayed them. When I look at these Indians, I feel like I'm looking at the face of America."

As he was honored by the Rosebud Sioux Tribal Nation in what is known as the Hunka Ceremony, an elder member of the Native American nation stated, "We are proud to adopt Kevin Costner as a brother... an honor we are bestowing upon him for his outstanding representation of our nation."

As thanks for the sensitive portayal of their people, the Sioux adopted him as a brother of Sinte Gleska College. Sinte Gleska is where Costner and his crew completed a crash course in Lakota, the Sioux language. The college is on the Rosebud Reservation in Rapid City, South Dakota. Mary McDonnell and Jim Wilson were also adopted by the Sioux Nation.

In turn, Costner returned his appreciation by donating $120,000 to create a permanent Sioux Indian exhibit at the South Dakota Cultural Heritage Center in Pierre. Costner and his wife donated the money in gratitude for the wonderful and welcome reception they received by the people of South Dakota while making the film there. Among other renderings, the exhibit will include a depiction of the rise and fall of the Ghost Dance, the forced retreat of the Sioux and their transition to reservation life.

What the critics thought about

DANCES WITH WOLVES

In THE NEW YORKER (Pauline Kael)
"It's a middle-of-the-road epic. This is a nature-boy movie, a kid's daydream of being an Indian. The movie – Costner's debut as a director – is childishly naive.... There isn't even anything with narrative power or bite to it. This Western is like a New Age social-studies lesson. It isn't really revisionist; it's the old stuff toned down and sensitized.... There's nothing affected about Costner's acting or directing. You hear his laid-back, surfer accent; you see his deliberate goofy faints and falls, and all the closeups of his handsomeness. This epic was made by a bland megalomaniac. (The Indians should have named him Plays With Camera.) You look at that untroubled face and know he can make everything lightweight.... Crowds of moviegoers love the movie, though – maybe partly because the issues have been made so simple.... Maybe also the crowds love this epic because it's so innocent: Costner shows us his bare ass like a kid at camp feeling one with the great outdoors. He's the boyish man of the hour: the Sioux onscreen revere him, because he's heroic and modest, too. TV interviewers acclaim him for the same qualities. He's the Orson Welles that everybody wants – Orson Welles with no belly."

In NEWSWEEK (David Ansen)
"*Dances With Wolves* is vulnerable both to charges of sentimentality and anachronism – the hero exhibits a sensibility at times dubiously contemporary. But if one's mind sometimes balks, one's heart embraces the movie's

fine, wide-open spirit, its genuine respect for a culture we destroyed without a second thought.... It's an engrossing tale, and Costner directs with the confidence of a Hollywood veteran well aware that entertainment comes before earnestness. He has a showman's instinct for mixing violence, humor and romance, a painterly eye for epic landscapes and an almost anthropological appreciation of the Sioux people.... Costner is no less shrewd serving himself up: like Robert Redford, he understands that understatement and a touch of self-mockery enhance his appeal."

In THE NEW REPUBLIC (Stanley Kauffmann)
"Michael Blake did the screenplay, and (two crucial points) Costner got Dean Semler as cinematographer and Neil Travis as editor. Those colleagues have helped the novice director to produce a picture that holds us by what it shows even when it lags in what it tells."

For the final word on *Dances With Wolves* I turn to the subject of this book himself. Kevin Costner has written the introduction to a book published by Newmarket Press on the making of the movie entitled *Dances With Wolves*. Michael Blake, Kevin Costner and Jim Wilson share credit for the book, whose purpose in revealing the picture's behind-the-scenes details is to "reflect the spirit and care that went into the making of *Dances With Wolves*."

Costner's introduction to the book seems the definitive statement of his feelings towards this experience in his life:

"*Dances With Wolves* is first and foremost a movie, and should be seen as one. The value of this book will never measure up to the first time you experience the movie. Since I know the story, I will forever be jealous of the pureness in which you are able to approach it and see it.

"With that in mind and off my chest, I can tell you that *Dances With Wolves* was in fact born out of a personal challenge, the seed of which came out of a conflict that could have easily torn the fabric of a long friendship. It will forever be to Michael Blake's credit that *Dances* was conceived and my great luck to be associated with it.

"*Dances* as a story began as most stories, with one writer confronting an empty piece of paper. There was no premise. There was no deadline. And out of this freedom came the opportunity to write from the heart.

"That Michael would write about the American frontier was in many ways a complete surprise. That I loved it was not. Michael managed to forge all the elements most attractive to me – simplicity, dignity, humor, and poignancy. He created a story that embraced a culture that has traditionally been misrepresented, both historically and cinematically.

"That *Dances* was a movie was clear. Whether I should direct this movie was probably the biggest question. It became both a personal and a professional battle. The one thing I knew, however, was that if *Dances* in the smallest way was not as great as movies that had shaped my love of them, I would always regret my decision.

"My only hope is that this movie has an impact on you. It wasn't made to manipulate your feelings, to reinvent the past, or to set the historical record straight. It's a romantic look at a terrible time in our history, when expansion in the name of progress brought us very little and, in fact, cost us deeply.

"This book represents the last physical responsibility

that I have to the movie, and through it I can reflect on the new friends that were made and the old that stood by me. I think how I have grown up, and now know more than ever the value of my family and the love of my friends.

"If I am blessed with good health, there is little doubt that I will make other movies, but if I could not, *Dances With Wolves* would complete the picture I have had of myself since I was a little boy. It will forever be my love letter to the past."

CHAPTER

7

ROBIN HOOD:

PRINCE OF THIEVES

The success of *Robin Hood: Prince Of Thieves* was a double-edged sword for Kevin Costner. Due to on-the-set tension and stress during the film's production, he and director Kevin Reynolds are no longer friends, and have become embittered towards one another. In addition, Costner's tyrannical behavior on the set earned him unflattering comparisons to Orson Welles.

Problems plagued the project from the minute Costner signed on to remake the 1938 MGM classic for Morgan Creek Productions. Costner chose to do this film for two reasons: friendship and money. His friend Kevin Reynolds had been assigned to direct the originally $30 million budgeted picture, for which Costner was paid $8 million. In committing to the project, Costner explained, "I'm doing it because he's [Reynolds] doing it."

When word of competing "Robin Hood" projects reached 20th Century Fox Chairman Joe Roth, he was furious. Roth had spent months of studio time and money on developing a "Robin Hood" film with director John McTiernan. To his chagrin, he discovered that two rival film companies "acted unjustly, if not immorally, by rushing competing 'Robin Hood' films into production when Fox was first," as he stated in *Variety*.

McTiernan had been signed to direct the Fox version from a Mark Allen Smith script entitled "The Adventures Of Robin Hood." An October date was set for McTiernan to begin filming. However, both Morgan Creek Productions and TriStar announced in July of 1990 that they too would be filming remakes of the 1938 Errol Flynn movie. Tri-Star was making *Robin Hood* and Morgan Creek was filming *Robin Hood: Prince Of Thieves*. Both were set to roll before the cameras on the third of September.

At that time, none of the three competing projects had firm commitments from any star to play the lead role. Mel Gibson, Patrick Swayze, Alec Baldwin, Kevin Kline and Kevin Costner were all being considered as contenders. The race was on because producers, and the Hollywood agencies involved, knew that whoever was the first to sign a major star would have the biggest jump on the competition. Having a well-known male lead signed to one role might make the others reconsider running against them head-on in a competing film role.

(Later, Costner would explain that Mel Gibson turned down the role because of its similarity to his character in *Hamlet*, another classic about an English hero in tights.)

The most persistent rumor at the time was that Costner was discussing the projects at both Fox and Morgan Creek. However, Morgan Creek had chosen Reynolds as director. Reynolds was Costner's friend and associate dating from the time of their work on *Fandango* and the two had remained close since. For that reason, it was widely speculated that Costner, if motivated to play the role, would choose Morgan Creek.

Roth continued to decry what he considered to be the underlying lack of morality displayed by the two competing studios who rushed projects into production against his. In *Variety*, Roth admitted that although the story was certainly public domain, he felt his colleagues were "exhibiting a lack of morality by going after the same piece of classic literature. If Disney, Warner or anyone else had a public domain script, I would not do this." As an independent producer before taking the reins at Fox, however, Roth soon found that there were many who feel his views on competitive productions in Hollywood are naive and out of sync with the realities of filmmaking. Others speculated Roth's anger stemmed from "nervousness" over the product of the opposition.

"I grew up understanding that competition meant you do the best you can – but by playing straight," Roth said in his own defense. The comments seem to ignore the fact that Hollywood has never "played it straight" when it comes to trying to capitalize on the successful product of the opposition. Shirley Temple, Marilyn Monroe and even Rin Tin Tin had their imitators in the form of clones offered by the competition to make a quick dollar. Why else would anyone ever think the brittleness of Jane Mansfield could substitute for the softness of Marilyn Monroe? In fact, this year, two competing "Christopher Columbus" films are being rushed into production against one another in order to capitalize on the 500th anniversary of the Italian sailor's voyage to America.

Following the successes of his *The Hunt For Red October*, *Die Hard* and *Predator*, McTiernan also became upset. "This has been a very stinging experience and it won't ever happen again. We finished the script two years ago and made a mistake in letting people know about it. People have went out and made sequels to my last three films [mentioned above] so I guess sooner or later I should have expected people would try to make a sequel to one of my films simultaneously," the director said sarcastically, adding that in order to avoid any possible incidents like this from occurring again in the future, he will register his scripts and projects under assumed names.

Added to these three competing projects later was a fourth, Turner Entertainment's release of the definitive *Robin Hood*, Warner Brothers' 1938 Technicolor smash, *The Adventures Of Robin Hood*.

Roth claimed that David Nicksay, now production president of the independent film company Roth founded, Morgan Creek, and producers Ed Zwick and Marshall Herskovitz, the producer and director respectively of the Tri-Star version, were "fully aware that Fox' 'Robin Hood' preceded theirs." Zwick responded to the press by saying, "I know Joe Roth and like him have never or would ever act unethically in business. His suggestion that our behavior is immoral is both hurtful and offensive." Roth countered, "regardless of the tack they're taking, they're still all making Robin Hood. For a man as professionally tied in as Zwick is, he understands the effect on the public that one 'Robin Hood' has on another when it hits the screen."

Not everyone agrees with Roth about this negative effect on audience reaction. When a film is a box office success, it only draws more people into theaters. Patrons often choose to see some alternate selection. Christmas releases are often better served at the box office when two or three big hit films are released. This makes many more people in the mood to be at theaters, and, as a result, they will often end up seeing something they did not expect to view when their first choice is unavailable to them.

Therefore, if you like "Robin Hood" and see one successful film about it, you are more than likely going to be willing to see another good "Robin Hood" picture. In today's market, how can one have "too many" good films from which to choose? The problem is the films that are made have to be good to keep generating additional audience interest. However, if one version of the production is a bomb and the filmgoer sees it first, he may decide not to attend other productions of it.

Still, Roth was also furious about a lesser-known

element of the "Robin Hood" competition. The William Morris Agency, which represents McTiernan and screenwriter Mark Allen Smith, also handles Peter Densham and John Watson, who drafted the screenplay for *Thieves*. Densham and Watson were set to produce *Thieves* for Morgan Creek with Trilogy Productions partner Richard B. Lewis. The sale of the script was completed earlier that year in February for the hefty sum of $1.2 million, ending a heated bidding war.

William Morris had no comment on the issue, but as usual, Roth did. "The Morris office clearly knew we were doing 'Robin Hood' at Fox when they made the deal," he groused. The competition finally died away, and seemingly, so did the other two 'Robin Hood' films (neither critical nor box-office successes) the minute Kevin Costner signed with Morgan Creek and Kevin Reynolds.

Morgan Creek executive David Nicksay waxed enthusiastic over the signing of Reynolds. "The thrilling thing about getting Kevin Reynolds is we think he's the perfect director to make this picture. He has a great sense of humor, a fantastic eye and an energetic shooting style. The minute we got him, we put him on a plane to London to get the production on its feet," he said.

Reynolds was hired by the producers on the strength of his less than successful 1988 film, *The Beast*. Reynolds being hired to direct this $30 million film, even with two box office failures behind him, is typical of an ever increasing trend by Hollywood film producers – hiring screenwriters and directors at huge salaries that have not been successful in returning a profit on previous films. It shows many producers will take the word of mouth about talent without looking into the track record of their past work.

This lack of homework by producers results in ever-escalating budgets for talent that does not have a successful history of returning their films' costs. When only one out of ten films returns its negative costs from U.S. and Canadian distribution, it is time producers learned to select individuals who know what the mass audience is looking for in entertainment that is not only creative but also financially responsible.

Indeed, spending $60 million on a film by a director who has not had a box office hit seems like faulty judgement on an already risky venture. At this point in time, *Thieves'* U.S. and Canadian gross is $164,000,000. This means that the rentals (the amount studios and profit participants share) account for approximately $80 million.

As Wall Street analysts have noted, the film must make $90 million for Morgan Creek to see a penny of profits. From overseas distribution and video and television rights, the film will bring in a nice-sized profit. However, with this analysis, one can see that it is hardly the box office smash it is reputed to be – especially since the original $30 million budget ballooned to $60 million plus, with advertising and "print" costs that raise the amount to the $90 million mentioned by Wall Street analysts.

The film was created around one of the largest marketing, merchandising and distribution plans ever. At one point, it was playing on more than 4,500 screens in the U.S. and Canada and at more than 2,000 overseas.

There are a bevy of merchandising/licensing deals associated with the film and the soundtrack from the film signals the first album release from the newly-created Morgan Creek Records. Michael Kamen did the instrumental score and Bryan Adams' first single in five years was the film's (Everything I Do) I Do It For You. The soundtrack went top 10 on Billboard's Top Pop Albums chart, and the single climbed to number one.

The marketing campaign for *Thieves* was also innovative in that special commercials were made for different target audiences. For women, the romance element was highlighted. For teen audiences, action and mysticism were the focus in advertising geared towards them.

Additionally, there were Warner Brothers merchandising deals for a Nintendo game, two novelizations, sleeping bags, clothing apparel, trading cards, party goods and small promotional items like mugs and buttons relating to the film. A Taco Bell tie-in was also highly anticipated for generating extra film revenues.

The movie marked another first. For the first time ever, Warner Brothers charged for all its films a minimum of $5 for adults and $3 for children in major markets and $4 and $2, respectively, in smaller markets. The primary motivation given for the new higher minimums was as insurance against exhibitors who discount price their product.

Thieves was set to shoot on September 3 at Shepperton Studios in London, the same studio where Sigourney Weaver tackled her "Gorillas in the Mist." The film's producers felt England was the best location, giving the film a true and dynamic sense of historical accuracy. They also felt the historical locations would lend the film a larger-than-life and true-to-life feel at the same time. The film's technical crew included Oscar-winning art director Alan Tomkins (*The Empire Strikes Back*) and Oscar-winning set decorator Peter Young (*Batman*), who gave the movie a 90's modernized feel insisted upon by the producers and Costner, who felt the story inherently leant itself to modernization.

"We're not going to mock the legend of 'Robin Hood,' but we will play with it sometimes," said its star. "We've added one or two things. For example, Robin has been in the Crusades and was captured and held for five years. So he isn't the carefree rascal Errol Flynn was."

One of the major hassles the "ghost" of Errol Flynn created for Kevin Costner was the formidable presence of those forest green tights worn by Flynn in the 1938 story. Costner refused to wear the tights for the filming, even though it was reported he "has the legs" for it. In the privacy of his own home, Costner says he tried the tights on for size and then made his decision. On the first day of fittings, as a joke, costume designer John Bloomfield had bright forest green tights and a jaunty little felt cap with a large feather awaiting him. Costner did a double take and the wardrobe designer panicked and left quickly.

"His courage didn't last too long," said Costner. Hollywood male stars are so afraid of hose that some dropped out of the running merely due to anxiety over the tights. The funny thing is that there is no actual proof recorded anywhere that Robin Hood ever wore green tights.

Costner opted for trousers of medieval brown and brought his own personal hairdresser to England. He worked with a dialect coach for several weeks but decided not to affect a British accent. However, if you listen closely during the film, you can hear it come and go in Robin's speech, depending upon what scene he is in.

Costner wanted to significantly modify the elements that made that 1938 film a success. He is not impressed by the MGM picture many consider a timeless piece of film craftsmanship and two hours of nonstop action, adventure and romance. "I admire Errol Flynn for being so good in such a silly movie," he stated.

Yet, the inevitable comparisons between Costner and Flynn must be made and I don't believe anyone, for all Flynn's flaws, could honestly say Costner's modern version is an improvement. In a recent newspaper poll on who was the "best" Robin Hood, the report went something like this: "Flynn's Merry Men were by far the merriest, while his fake castles looked far more real than the real castles used in the Costner epic. But nobody, it was decided, could match the matchlessly handsome drunk [Flynn] for hands-on-hips laughter and devil-may-care attitude. There was, however, a sympathy vote for the clunky-but-rich Costner, who was saddled with lines that Richard Burton sober couldn't have carried off."

Another example of how the story was modernized was the addition to the cast of Christian Slater as Will Scarlett. His modern-day attitude and look helped lessen Costner's miscasting and his role added some of the little flair the film possessed. Yet his inclusion was one more sign of the obsession on the part of the filmmakers to ensure that their story was not "outmoded." Robbing from the rich and giving to the poor will not be "outmoded" as long as there continue to be rich and poor. Still, the tendency of many of today's executives of including "everything but the kitchen sink" (even if it doesn't fit into the period or plct) in their films as insurance for returning their investment is exactly what clutters so many of our films today and often renders their plot incoherent. Nicksay promised Slater would "bring a fresh attitude to the character of Will Scarlett," but is it necessary, or cinematically believable on the other hand, to give a universally appealing character from the 12th century the attitude of a James Dean?

The filmmakers also added a Moor to the story in the person of Morgan Freeman, whom critic Pauline Kael has called "maybe the finest actor in America." Freeman plays Azeem, a Moor with a distaste for the British who nonetheless rescues Robin from death at the hands of the enemy. Freeman is painted for this role, even though the Koran forbids any kind of body decoration. The role "ticked off" Freeman because "it should have come sooner, like when I was 15. In Mississippi, where I grew up, I used to get up and not stop running till after midnight. I'm a little beyond it now, but not so beyond it that I can't do it."

Costner numbered Freeman as one of the primary reasons for doing *Thieves*. "He gives the story a nice spin," he explained.

Freeman, meanwhile, defends Costner against charges of egomaniacal behavior. He says, "Kevin's giving, he's real, he's there, he's honest, he's available. If you're working with an actor, you don't want to hear 'Just a second' when you need to talk to him. You've got Kevin's immediate attention. There's no in-between people separating the lord and master from the great unwashed. He's one guy who's taken his success in stride."

The filming was often cold and wet and Costner tried, as usual, to keep his family involved with him during his career activities. This time Costner's parents stayed home, but Cindy Costner visited the set one day to find her husband exercising what leverage he could in his quarter staff battle against Little John.

Instead of being a lark for her, Cindy could only worry once again about her husband's dangerous stunts. Her visit was filled mostly with visions of her husband being hit on his torso over and over again until he is knocked into the freezing river water. Cindy tried to influence the duration of the scene by giving Reynolds the cold shoulder. "I felt that me standing there glaring at the director would have more impact," she said. "I thought Kevin might accomplish the scene in three or four takes this way instead of seven or eight takes."

By the fourth day of the water-plunging activities, Cindy finally had her husband reveal to her in the privacy of their own room that he was "really scared to go back in the water" and that he "couldn't sleep that night." One should not consider Costner a coward – the waters he was being plunged into were the 100-m.p.h. torrents of Aysgarth Falls in North Yorkshire.

One amusing incident is that the water was so cold that Costner, who has given us bare buttocks shots in *Revenge* and *Dances With Wolves*, had a double stand in for this, the third full-derriere shot in as many films.

By November, the Costner family joined him on the set for Thanksgiving, holding the celebration on a date before the actual one in order to give the actor the freedom to complete filming.

Increasingly, however, the film's director saw little reason for thanksgiving, and soon a major battle between the two Kevins occurred over the editing of the film. The recent Oscar-winner for Best Director has been labeled a "500-pound gorilla" in Hollywood circles after prevailing in disputes over the three-hour scope of his *Dances With Wolves* and getting his way on the set of *Thieves*.

An article in the "Buzz" column of *Variety* reported, "don't expect [the pair] to work together again after numerous clashes on *Robin Hood: Prince of Thieves*. They supposedly had a 'creatively unfulfilling experience.'"

Those close to the pair reported Costner felt Reynolds was closed to outside input and Reynolds resented Costner's continual attempts to direct the film. At one point, Costner got behind the camera and directed some shots, and at times it was reported there were always two Kevins looking into the monitors. A final hostile editing battle between the pair had Costner coming down on the side of executives. The disagreement has for now wedged a rift in their professional association and off-set friendship (Reynolds was one of the buffalo wranglers on *Dances With Wolves*).

The filming took one hundred days and went one week over schedule. Due to the rush to get it before audiences, Reynolds admits, "We were ready to be fried before Christmas."

Reynolds, a lawyer before attending the University of Southern California film school, said that "the only advantage of my law education is that I am much less likely to get bamboozled by the business guys." As a kid who grew up in Texas and New Mexico, he saw movies as "a dream world, too remote and inaccessible to think about approaching. Honest, I had no *idea* that one day I'd be here doing this."

After *The Beast* failed miserably, Reynolds spent three years in development hell. Before tensions forced Costner to seize control of the direction and editing on the set of "Thieves," he had nothing but good to say about his friend as director. "I have a lot of faith in Kevin. He'll be one of our greatest American directors. But faith is a funny thing. It can get to the point where everyone figures the director doesn't need help – 'Oh, he'll pull it out of the hat' – which is a tough situation to put someone in. On *Dances*, I was pretty much on my own."

The mounting tensions on the set were not helped any by the fact that the budget ballooned from $30 million to $60 million by the end of shooting. Additionally, the role of Maid Marian had to be recast when actress Robin Wright became pregnant.

Bad weather created delays in shooting and forced the entire reshooting of one scene while the Sherwood Forest scenes had to be hurried before the autumn leaves fell. Meanwhile, the constant English drizzle left everyone with one sort of cold or another. At the last minute, Sean Connery was hired to do a half-day's cameo for the princely sum of half a million dollars.

Costner has defended his actions about having final word in the conflicts between Kevin Reynolds and himself. He feels he must be responsible for more than his performance because "the risks I take in this business are personal, not professional. Professionally, I'll always be able to go on and make another movie. Personally, I just don't want to make a bad movie. Professionally, it would all be forgotten eventually. Personally, I'd never forget it. I take things really personally."

However, Costner's assessment that he can always "go on and make another movie" may prove short-sighted, considering the fickleness of audiences. Audiences have seldom traditionally followed a director or actor "anywhere" they go. What they have done is pay to go where they want, but they pay who they want to take them there. When someone takes them to fun places, like Disney or Spielberg, they are more willing to follow (i.e., pay their ticket costs). In light of this, Costner should realize that there are no guarantees personally or professionally, except giving the audience what they like with someone they like. Audiences may like Costner, but he should remember they have not always followed him, as evidenced by the box-office failures *Fandango, American Flyers, Silverado* and *No Way Out*). Scripts that are universal and warm like *Dances With Wolves* and *Robin Hood: Prince Of Thieves* may heighten Costner's chances of always being one of the stars with whom audiences would prefer to share their cinema experiences.

So has the "good guy" turned into an Orson Welles-like dictator after his Oscar success? (Sources say Costner regards himself more like Louis B. Mayer.) *"Robin Hood: Prince of Thieves* was not a perfect situation for me," he said in reference to his taking control of the direction. "If this movie has any trouble later on, what a nice angle: 'Kevin Costner took the reins and started directing himself.' This monster."

Still, Costner has long been known for being self-directed and a bit of an obsessive nit-picker on the set. He admits, "It's a hard line. I've probably, in a way, grown up more on this film than on any film. There are things I could not control on this movie that I think needed to be controlled. Two years ago, three years ago, in the privacy of my room, I'd go crazy, and I *still* go a little crazy, but I found that I'm able to show up every day and try. Just try."

Reynolds will only say in response to the problems: "When I first started, I used to yell a lot more." Costner has repeatedly stated that this film was his "least satisfying artistically."

Perhaps the film would have been more successful had the filmmakers adopted David O. Selznick's advice about adapting beloved legends for the screen. Selznick, perhaps Hollywood's most successful producer of adapted classics

(*A Tale Of Two Cities, David Copperfield, Gone With The Wind*), cautioned "GWTW" screenwriter Sidney Howard about adaptation in a memo: "I certainly urge most strongly against including any sequence [of our invention] in which Rhett is shown 'doing his stuff' as a blockade runner. We will be forgiven for cuts if we do not invent sequences."

Maybe I am alone in my sensibilities, but I cannot believe Selznick would have allowed any writer to invent a Maid Marian that punches Robin in the "balls." In addition, Maid Marian has been given a "new woman" responsibility by having to defend her family's land while England's men were away conducting the Crusade.

Regardless of its box office success, critics in general ripped the film apart. Tired of the star's sanctimonious self-promotion (the same traits which made him refer to his own "boyish enthusiasm" as he accepted his Oscar) reviewers treated the picture much as Madonna treated Costner in *Truth or Dare* – by sticking her fingers down her throat and mock-gagging.

The movie, called everything from jumbled to laughable, had critics chiding Costner for taking control of the direction and turning the vehicle into a monument to his own star ego.

John Powers, remarking on the egomaniacal behavior prevalent in Hollywood, said, "I refuse to believe he's starring in a $200 million adaptation of "Ozymandius").

Still, "sticks and stones" may break Costner's bones, but no harsh words from critics have harmed the film's mass audience appeal.

What the critics said about

ROBIN HOOD: PRINCE OF THIEVES

In TLS (Tom Shippey)

"...does not compare with the other popular films such as Star Wars in its sense of an unfamiliar but consistent technology lurking in the background like it could have done. Take bows, for instance. The Robin Hood legends took shape during the few generations when people like Chaucer's Knight's Yeoman – 'And in his hand he baar a myghty bowe' – were death to their social superiors on the battlefields of Europe. And mighty was the word for them. The pull on a six-foot armour-piercing yew bow might be double that of a competition bow today. To judge from the skeletons of the 'Mary Rose's' archer-crewman, to shoot one you needed a barrel chest, permanently-thickened forearm bones from incessant practice in adolescence, and a spine twisted clockwise by the pressures of the terrible pull. Kevin Costner's bows look like Dinky toys. They are shot usually at fifteen yards' range, which is a good job, as half the archers are holding their arrows between finger and thumb, thus restricting their draw-weight to the strength of the weakest digit. The catapults we see wouldn't work, either. Azeem, it is true, introduces the telescope and gunpowder (so much for Friar Bacon), but the latter at least is a cop-out. All this is failure of imagination. And though the film is redolent with appeals to cultural relativism and equal validity for everything, the one culture it has no respect for is the one it is about. It makes our ancestors look like fools. Innocently, I grant. But would that do as a defense these days for patronizing images of alien contemporary cultures?"

In THE SPECTATOR (Harriet Waugh)
"...Robin and Marian's courtship is embarrassing. A child –
and this is a children's film – would consider it boring and
slushy and the dialogue never rises above that of a comic
book. On the other hand, the action scenes are bloody and
exciting and the climax in which the outlaws take on the
Sheriff of Nottingham has some startling effects, one of the
funniest and more macabre being the literally last-minute
attempt of the Sheriff to rape Maid Marian.

It is quite likely that Robin Hood never existed and even
if he did, he was certainly not the folk hero that we tell about
now. Given these facts, it is difficult to understand why the
American critics got into such a lather about the film,
accusing it of being boringly politically correct."

In SIGHT & SOUND (John Powers)
"Costner has obviously hit on a formula for success in the
new decade. Both *Robin Hood: Prince of Thieves* and *Dances
With Wolves* preserve the simple-minded formulas of the
Reagan-era cinema (triumphant individualism,
unmistakable distinctions between good and evil, a
hectoring manipulation of feeling that allows only one
response). Yet they invest them with the most fashionable
'progressive' notions of the early 90's (ecological sanity,
celebration of victimized Native Americans, robbing from
the rich to give to the poor, New Age notions of personal
growth).

Although I remain skeptical about Costner's sincerity
(he privately makes campaign contributions to right-wing
politicians), I must concede that his movies are perfectly
suited to the Bush years. Benevolently retrograde, they offer
Reaganism with a human face – which, to judge from the

frequency with which they are bared, looks remarkably like Costner's twinkling buttocks. *Robin Hood: Prince of Thieves*, it should be added, is every bit as fuddled as our ex-President. This is one reason why every critic I know is depressed by its huge popularity: the movie serves up big budget film-making at its most slipshod, but the audience doesn't seem to care or notice."

Upon close examination of the box office, however, one sees John Powers is incorrect in thinking the audience "doesn't seem to notice or care" about "slipshod" filmmaking. As already noted, *Thieves'* huge box office success in the U.S. and Canada was still barely enough to justify its enormous costs. In other words, the slipshod nature of the film more than likely held it back from making even more profit at the box office, so the audience does care and notice.

At the same time, in today's often dour film environment, you cannot blame people for wanting some harmless and unthreatening family-oriented entertainment with a good old-fashioned action-adventure and love story plot. That the film symbolizes just this, in a time when motion pictures strive to have a "social conscience" (i.e., bore us with their artistic pretensions and pseudo-intellectualism) explains more than anything the universal appeal and box-office success behind *Thieves*.

One last interesting note about the film. In New Orleans, while working on the set of *JFK*, Costner heard about a young boy with terminal cancer who wanted to view *Thieves* but was afraid he would die before having the chance. Costner invited the lad to a sneak preview of the film and sat next to him the entire viewing. Sean Dunlap, 14, said he "was looking forward to the film but it wasn't opening until June 14 and he wouldn't be here that long." A sneak preview was held in suburban Metairie on June 1. A week later, Sean was dead.

It is perhaps the therapeutic and uplifting element of films that should inspire actors, directors and producers to choose films that lift the spirit and add hope to the human condition. Robin Hood is one such character.

For a final word, as Costner himself admitted about the story, "the very idea of Robin Hood brings a smile to your face. The idea that people can fight back when wealthy people abuse them is something everybody responds to. We all rally around the theme of the underdog."

CHAPTER

8

TIG PRODUCTION CO.
& REVENGE

Kevin Costner and Jim Wilson are partners in Tig Production Company, a film production company christened with Costner's grandmother's nickname. In the summer of 1989, the company was formed, and by 1990, Tig Production Company signed an exclusive deal with Orion Pictures.

Under the terms of the negotiations, the pair entered into a long-term arrangement whereby Costner will produce and/or star in a number of major films for the studio via his Tig Production Company. *Dances With Wolves* was produced by Costner and Wilson, but it was produced and financed independently under contract with Orion. However, Orion was the domestic distributor.

Costner was enthusiastic about the deal because he felt the executives at Orion Pictures had artistic sensibilities. He stated at the time, "I have made Orion my creative home [because] of the enormously satisfying experience I had making *No Way Out* and *Bull Durham*." He praised the company for the autonomy it allowed its filmmakers as well as "its skills in marketing and distribution." All of the films will be under the Tig name and released worldwide by Orion and produced or co-produced by Costner's longtime associate Jim Wilson.

The pair immediately solidified their relationship with writers, directors and actors in order to meet their lofty goal of two productions a year. Costner joins the studio's current roster of big-name talent, including Woody Allen, Jonathan Demme, Dennis Hopper and Dennis Quaid. Eric Pleskow, Orion President, said "Orion's success has been based on its long-term relationships with extraordinary individuals. Kevin is one of today's finest actors and most popular film stars. He is also a man with great creative insights in all areas of the filmmaking process."

After the success of *Dances With Wolves*, scripts started to pile up at Tig Production almost as quickly as dollars. Costner now has virtual *carte blanche* from every studio in town. Says Michael Blake: "Make no mistake, he and Jim Wilson are the top 'tag team' in the movies today."

Eric Pleskow goes on to add, "Kevin can direct for Orion any time" while Larry Gordon, a veteran producer and sometime studio chief, is more direct. "Kevin Costner is one of those people who's so wonderful you hope to God he never changes. Any movie he wants to make, I'll be there."

The first two films Tig Production slated for production were *Mick* and *American Sportsman*. *Mick* is a film based on the life of Irish revolutionary Michael Collins and is set to star Costner. The film is written by Eoghan Harris and Robert Dillion. Tom Johnston is Executive Producer. Orion is to fully finance the picture and retain all worldwide rights.

The producers are aware that *Mick* is not going to be inexpensive because it is a period film, set in the early part of this century. *Mick* is a project that has been around. In 1987, Harris' screenplay was set to be directed by Michael Cimino and produced by Nelson Entertainment for $18 million. Columbia was set to distribute the picture then, and Cimino got as far as active preproduction – with location cameras set to roll on July 1, 1987 – before the project was shelved.

The property landed at Orion after Columbia passed on it. Wilson says the picture is a "sweeping epic, a love story" set during the Easter Uprising of 1916 and resulting struggle for a Free State in 1920's-era Ireland. The film will focus on the controversial life of Collins, a legendary Irish hero who was later assassinated.

American Hero, on the other hand, is also a Kevin Costner-starring vehicle but no development plans other than that have been made. Costner laughs at the notion that so-called great ideas are enough to make a great film. In a speech to independent filmmakers in Los Angeles, he noted, "I'm so sick of great ideas. I am almost as sick of great ideas as I am sick of great stories that are very involved. Neither one of those things necessarily makes a great movie. Hard work makes a movie, and the hardest thing of all is a good script... The ability not to fool yourself will serve you better than any quality or talent you might have – or lack."

Often, people will hear that in Hollywood you cannot be an independent producer and get very far due to studio control. Costner feels nothing could be more false. He feels there is every opportunity in the world for a good script and hard-working people. Says he: "The battle of the independent is not with the studio. The perception could never be that they don't want you. This is clearly a business that makes room for good people. "The battle that exists is with yourself – and with myself. It's our ability to face the facts, to face reality. The reality is that if you're good, they cannot keep you out... There is nothing covert. Is there a secret group keeping the independents down? There is no secret group." Costner should well know, as he and co-producer Jim Wilson had to take their independent production of *Dances With Wolves* overseas to find backing. It was truly an independent's success story that went against the traditional studio methods and stories.

Costner further asserted that it is the individual who makes a difference and not an anonymous "group" of people trying to stop success for others.

"There is no 'they,' " Costner said. "The 'they' is you.

The problems that exist for me... Where is the good material? Where are the scripts? For a business that cloaks itself in creativity, it's an almost monotonous question we go through. It's the one constant... The magic (is) reading a script alone at night after having waded through 50, and suddenly the pages turn faster than before. You find yourself rushing through, hoping that the last 30 pages are as good as the first 90." This lack of quality writing for the screen is one of the biggest problems with our films today, which are incoherent, implausible and with otherwise unintelligible scripts.

Where acting projects are concerned, Costner feels ensemble pictures are best for success. "If I had my druthers, I'd rather fit into an ensemble. I don't look for pictures for Tig for the leads. The fact that I get some leads, you can derive what you want from that, but that's not my intention, because it ain't an easy thing to do. You take all the heat. You're usually the straight man, unless you're in an action picture. I guess what can happen is people know I can turn a line, and I can sustain a performance. I have notions about my characters. And I believe in the movie experience, I understand it and I know what my job as lead is."

Costner also had the following to say about his feelings on "leading men" and what he looks for when picking projects for Tig:

"The thing about a leading man is you have to like him. You have to want to look at him for a long period of time. He can't be too interesting, too distracting, because the supporting actors are the ones who have to be interesting. I'm a good leading man because I don't need support." Costner seems at times to possess a multitude of contradictions.

Things seemed to be going well for Orion Pictures where Kevin Costner was concerned. Both studio and star shared a mutual respect. In addition, Costner and partner Jim Wilson had their exclusive contract and were ready to put the two mentioned films into production. Costner was also set to star. The actor had already made *No Way Out* and *Bull Durham*, huge hits for the studio. To add to their good fortune, the film they distributed from Costner's first directing effort, *Dances With Wolves*, made him one of the most successful and most famous people in the world – not to mention opening the magic "financing" doors for him at any studio in town. Then the bomb dropped.

In March of 1991, due to his involvement with three films shooting there, Kevin Costner was frequently in the office given to him at Warner Brothers. The three films *Robin Hood: Prince Of Thieves*, Oliver Stone's *JFK* and the currently-filming *The Bodyguard* all were shot within one year's time. Rumors were rampant that partners Costner and Wilson were fleeing the cash-poor Orion Pictures for Warner Brothers. Neither would comment on the move at the time, but if true, it would represent a major boon to Warner Brothers, which was low in talent. (Costner's earlier *Fandango* and *American Flyers* were also filmed at Warner Brothers.)

Orion executives were privately outraged and publicly silent. How could Costner leave them when they needed him most, especially after they had given him a chance to do the two "baseball movies" nobody else in town wanted to risk touching?

It was not the first breach of loyalty to occur so early in a relationship, and ironically, it was Warner Brothers which had last been publicly ditched in a billion-dollar deal that sent shock waves through the Hollywood community.

An article in the May 20 *Variety* soon confirmed that partners Kevin Costner and Jim Wilson had indeed relocated their production facilities to the Warner Brothers lot. The new agreement gave Costner the right to direct, develop, produce and star in films for the studio. The first-look deal was signed with Tig Productions as Costner was beginning filming of *The Bodyguard*. Terms of the pact such as the number of pictures and duration of the commitment were not made known, but it is rumored that the deal was very similar to Mel Gibson's pact with the studio.

While Orion scored with *Dances With Wolves* and *The Silence Of The Lambs* at the box office (*Dances* brought in over $168 million in 185 days), they had to sell the *The Addams Family* to Paramount for quick cash. One story behind Costner's defection is that he is not seeing his *Dances With Wolves* profits due to Orion's cash troubles and near-bankruptcy. Costner was paid a mere $1.5 million to act in *Dances* but took a hefty piece of the gross for directing.

Meanwhile, *Variety* reported in July of 1991 that Costner is not receiving anywhere near his piece of the pie. So far he's received only $7.5 million from the studio and sources report that's not anywhere near what he's due. The estimates range closer to the estimated $50 million Jack Nicholson received from his participation in Warner Brother's smash *Batman*.

A spokesman for Costner denied the report, but *Variety* was adamant that Costner is "worried about being stalled and that his agent, Creative Artists Agency's head Mike Ovitz, has been putting the pressure on Orion to collect what's due."

Costner is reportedly "thrilled" with the Warner

Brothers alliance and says his deal with Orion covered the distribution of all his pictures but not his services as actor, which has led to the perception that this lack of loyalty or sympathy for Orion shows Costner meant it when he said, "Life is trying to eat all of us. And you either eat life or you're eaten." Despite the boyish reputation and demeanor and sounding more like an existential Social Darwinist than a Baptist, this is a man who means business.

Although Orion Pictures was left holding the bag when Costner abandoned ship, they still retain the rights to some lucrative Costner vehicles, including *Mick* and *American Hero*. Tig Productions has already produced *China Moon*, starring Ed Harris and to be released in 1992. Wilson stated that "any other projects that had been developed within Orion will be distributed by the company." Still, the enormous success and recognition of *Dances With Wolves* has been some salve to Orion's wounded ego.

In describing his approach at Warner Brothers, Costner again underscored the importance of a great script. He said good scripts are rarer today in Hollywood than any other element involved in a film's production. He felt this is because few will put the effort and care necessary into producing a good script. A good script is "the product of hard work, simple and clear. I will not quit until I find the person who had done that work, and try to be part of the dream with him... I think of the great script in terms of power bait."

The story behind the making of Kevin Costner's second film of 1989, *Revenge*, is included here because Costner executive-produced and helped write the script revisions with *Dances With Wolves* author and screenwriter Michael Blake. In addition, because he did not feel the production or writing were done well, he was characteristically outspoken about the tensions and roadblocks one faces when trying to get quality material from the page to the screen while pleasing studio executives at the same time.

Revenge is different for another reason. It is the first film role in which Costner plays a "bad" guy who steals another man's wife. The movie co-starred Anthony Quinn as the cuckolded husband and Madeleine Stowe as the disloyal wife. As Costner said about this film, which represented a change of pace for him: "*Revenge* is a movie that's right on the edge. Will people be really satisfied? I don't know because this movie ends in tragedy. It's not an 'up' ending. Maybe you won't even like me as a character."

Other than his sex scenes with Madeleine Stowe, audiences *didn't* and the film failed to return its costs. Costner knew before making it that this film might pose a problem for his image and said in defense of taking that risk, "I know that guys in the audience are going to be going, 'Cochran [Costner's character], oh, Jeez, oh no, man, don't do it,'. That's where you like people to be during a movie. So you stay and watch, but you're going, 'Oh, no.' Hey, it's the movies, and stuff happens." In spite of this reasoning, audiences proved by their lack of attendance at this film that with *married* women is *not* where they like their heroes to be.

In addition to its unusual story where Costner is concerned, *Revenge* had a history in Hollywood before Costner even became involved in the project. Previously, the newly-hired Columbia Studio head David Puttnam had sent powerful producer Ray Stark a memo that he wasn't exactly thrilled about this project. Major confrontation erupted and in the end Stark stayed while Puttnam departed. Costner was convinced Stark would drop his option after all the commotion, and, for a modest sum, allow him to buy it and direct. However, Stark held onto *Revenge* almost as firmly as Anthony Quinn tries to hang onto his wife in the film. Tony Scott, director of *Top Gun* and *Beverly Hills Cop*, also wanted to direct the project. The meeting between the three took place in Stark's office.

Costner recalls that he accepted Scott as the director "but I do think," he told Stark and Scott, "that everything has a right to be challenged." Stark and Scott didn't catch the full implication of Costner's statement until a few meetings later. Stark and Scott were thrilled and Costner reports, "everybody was really happy and ready to break out the champagne" but Costner was far from a partying mood. He said, "We still have a fucking problem here, boys. You're moving too slowly. If we don't pick up, I'm going to have to do 'Shoeless Joe' [the original title of *Field Of Dreams*] first. It was like pissing on the parade." It was also the truth and stated in typical Costner style – blunt.

Revenge is based on a Jim Harrison novella and tells the tight and muddy tale of an Air Force flyer who retires while in his mid-thirties. He befriends an older Mexican millionaire whose wife is young and wants a child.

The millionaire, who had guarded his wife's beauty more than he had her piety, soon learns of the betrayal and has his wife's face slashed before drugging her and sending her off to a brothel. Meanwhile, Costner's character fares little better when he is beaten to a near-fatal pulp. As director Scott says, "If there's a villain, it's love," which could be one reason so few people chose to see it. Who wants to pay money to find out even love can be a *villain*?

The character played by Costner is an Othello-type individual whose passion causes a fall from grace, the clue to the character, as far as the actor was concerned. He notes, "This is a guy who's liked and respected by other men. He's not a fighter jock with no background who sees a beautiful woman." Still, Costner is known to demand dialogue changes and this occasion was no different. He reported that as revision after revision failed to change his mind about the quality of the script, "what I found is, as each writer comes on, part of his getting credit and money depends on his rewriting everything. And so great moments were being thrown away. And the movie got pushed back. Finally, while I was shooting *Field Of Dreams*, I called up and said, 'This is the most awful script I've ever been connected to. It's equally as good a story as I've ever been part of.' I couldn't stand that shit, so I brought my friend Michael Blake out, and in 21 days, working between shots and on the way home in the car, we did a new script."

While the Costner-Blake revisions were not utilized, the star made his point. Scott did not mind the interference because he felt the changes Costner was pressing for were valid.

He notes, "Directors always resent when an actor wants to make changes – especially a few weeks before shooting. But when Kevin pushed for lean and mean changes, he was right."

At this time, Costner began to gain his now famous reputation of being Hollywood's new "Orson Welles." Liz Smith, the noted entertainment columnist, reported that Costner was becoming not only like Welles, but like Chaplin, Streisand and Hoffman as well. As she reported in her column during the filming of *Revenge*:

"There have always been a few actors who've taken creative control of their projects – off the top of my head I can think of Charlie Chaplin, Orson Welles, Robert Redford, Barbra Streisand. And Dustin Hoffman is famous, too, for having scripts rewritten and for being a perfectionist when it comes to details. So Kevin Costner is one of the latest to change his hand on the throttle. He allegedly rewrote large chunks of the script for his coming Ray Stark movie, *Revenge*. And Costner is now starring in and directing his own first feature film."

The script still never fully satisfied its lead player. Like Pirandello's six characters in search of an author, Costner reveals the different writers working on this project were still searching for a good script.

"The fact is that it was such a rich story that every writer was able to derive things out of it," he explained. "As it was rewritten, it got farther and farther away from what the book was. In the final analysis, what I tried to do was bring it back to what had attracted me and everyone to the book in the first place, which was that it's a story, a 99-page story."

The final script was credited to Harrison and Jeffrey Fiskin. Costner said it met his demands because of the type of actor he is. "I'm a real lean, linear kind of actor. I try to have forward motion in everything, where basically you just stand there and do your lines. You know what I mean? The lines will decide what is important," he asserted.

Scott also agreed with his star's approach. Noted the director, "I pushed them to give me this piece. Because I think I have a reputation for being a visual director and glitzy and rock and roll, not everybody was convinced in terms of giving me this material. It's different from what I have done. I suppose I loved it because it had a whole range of emotional buttons to push. It had passion, violence, and it's set in the strange world of Mexico, with those overwhelming locations, those beautiful landscapes." The film is beautifully realized and Costner spends a good deal of the time walking across the different landscapes silent.

Not only was Costner rewriting, he was complaining about the editing to anyone within earshot – and smoking words they were. He was most infuriated over a favorite scene of his that had been cut. It seemed he no longer accepted his "cut" scenes as gracefully as he once had from Lawrence Kasdan's "shears" on *The Big Chill*.

He was also irate over the inability to control what he thought was the shape the film should have taken. He said, "There's a scene that's cut out – I'm not even in it – that I miss. The wife asks Quinn for a baby and he gives her the Anthony Quinn deaf ear. The crudeness of that scene, that macho Latin hold on the woman – I care about that. A lot of people said it was vulgar. And I'd say, 'Why do you keep making my point?'"

Costner was also quite upset over the somewhat "happy" ending. He says there should have been an unhappy ending to justify the events in the story leading up to then. He feels it is a shame for the film and for audiences.

As he states, "And the end – look, this is one of the first movies about *violence*, how swift and mean and *ugly* it is, and how it spills over and affects a lot of other people. And in the end of that movie, the woman *should* die. Well, they shot it two ways. That's a fucking tragedy – the movie's a tragedy, and it's a tragedy that we shot it two ways. The film may still work, but those decisions screw around with the audience's confidence. I mean, the only way to know if you've seen a movie is if *all* the elements are there."

Costner was angry over not being able to see this film

turn out the way he thought it should be and he did not stop here. He also said that, "Listen to me – I sound like a big crab apple. I'm not. But those things are worth fighting for, they're *not* worth stopping the movie. I mean, it's not like 'Fuck you. I'm so far into this movie, everybody can walk. We'll see who wins.' I know the only power I have [as an actor] is the power of a good argument. I try to use that. The unfortunate thing is that a good argument is sometimes lost on who's got the guns." Or as a wise man once said, "do not teach a pig to sing, for it wastes your time and annoys the pig."

Costner had even more to express about his lack of control on a project he thought would have benefitted immensely from it, arguing that the unique structure and method of shooting a film can cause problems. "If the movie starts to slip away dramatically, there are certain things I can't control, even as executive producer," he said. "Movies always threaten to go somewhere else, not because someone is trying to do it on purpose, but because they are fragmented, that's the way they are shot. So you just become another eye looking out for the movie."

When he read the original script, Costner remembers there was one line in particular that, for him, made him feel an immediate connection to the character: "There is an impulse for vengeance among certain men south of the border that leaves even the sturdiest Sicilian gasping for fresh air." The actor even confessed that he "contemplated directing the film because it seemed like a small movie. The story was manageable, but the themes were big and universal, and the writing was tough and it was honest and it was original. There was poignance [his favorite script element] in the story, but it read like a movie to me."

Even though the production was fraught with stress and difficulty for him personally, it shows the type of man Costner can be that he rose above his personal feelings and showered his attentions – and gifts – among cast and crew. When he was making the film in Cuernavaca, Mexico, he worked with Luciana Cabarga, consul for movies, who remembered him for his generosity, down-to-earth manner and charm. "He was so considerate and generous to the staff, they still all talk about him – especially the women. He paid them well and was thoughtful about the hours they worked."

This is not the first time Costner has been generous nor is it likely to be the last. His Delta Chi frat brothers at California State University at Fullerton were also very impressed with their fellow frat brother's generous offer to host a benefit. For $50 a head, those in attendance were able to view *No Way Out* with the star, who dined and chatted with the young men. The event raised over $12,000 for the fraternity.

Another quality aspect of the *Revenge* shooting was that it gave Costner a chance to work with an actor he has great respect for – the legendary Anthony Quinn. Quinn was equally charmed by the young star, who reminds him of Gary Cooper. As Quinn says, "I really love that boy. He reminds me of my friend Gary Cooper. Coop was always looking for a place to spit and Kevin has that same puckered look."

Quinn took the film in stride after all his years and ups and downs in the film industry. He even joked about his role, saying, "I'm very happy to be in this picture. Because it is probably the last picture I'll ever do where I get to have a young wife." The location site for *Revenge* was somewhat of a homecoming for Quinn, who was born in Chihuahua at the height of the Mexican Revolution. (He was still a baby when he came to Los Angeles.)

Costner remarks that the Quinn persona was even more special to the meaning of the film than his. Quinn played Tiburon, also known as Tibey, and the casting of the role was not an easy challenge.

As Costner stated, "This movie needed Anthony Quinn more than it needed me. I mean, there are probably five or six guys who could play Cochran's role, but who else is there who could play the role of Tibey? The Tiburon character has to be really charming, and Anthony has that in spades. He has to have danger and he has to have presence. Anthony has that because he's been a leading man all his life. And he has to be that age. The age is key, so it's a perfect role for him."

Quinn himself went on to express that he found the role of Tiburon somewhat close to home. "I think the man is of another time and his values are of another time. It's the old country mentality, which also happens to be mine. I think sexual liberation is a lot of garbage. I mean, there's no code, there's no honor. It was a question of morality that Tiburon takes the action he does. So that's why I did this picture, that and the fact it's a classic old-fashioned story that could have been done by John Wayne or Gary Cooper."

Quinn, who turned 75 during the filming, says he first thought audiences might not accept him in the role of being married to such a younger woman. "I had my doubts," he reported. "Obviously, you know how old I am, and I didn't know if people would accept that I had such a young wife. I thought I should be 15, maybe 20 years younger. But I'm still a very physical man; even now I play an hour or two of tennis every day. I go walking. I exercise in the morning. I swim an awful lot. And I do see young girls looking at me, so I thought, what the hell."

The veteran actor went on to say that he felt the real heartbreak for his character did not come as much from the disloyalty of his wife as much as it did from the disloyalty of his friend. He said of the story, "Cochran doesn't know that my love for him is because he is my surrogate son. Sometimes we older men love a young man because we see in him qualities that we had or hoped to have. For my character, there's great pain in losing the wife, but that pain is not as great as losing the friend."

Quinn also felt his character might come across as too insensitive to women with a more of a "new world" attitude. He shared his feelings concerning their anticipated reaction to his character's "macho" actions: "I'm aware that a lot of American women will not understand my behavior, will find it as twisted as all hell. They'll say, 'Well, that terrible man, he slices up the girl's face and then almost kills his friend.' I'm saying that the man can't help it; he was born with that morality. I mean, a hunting dog can't help that it bites." Maybe a hunting dog *cannot* help it, but if he truly felt like it, a human being that does not wish to be a detriment to society *could*. As the Katharine Hepburn character reminds Mr. Allnut (the Humphrey Bogart role) in the *African Queen*: "Nature, Mr. Allnut, is what we're in this world to rise *above*."

Director Tony Scott took another interpretation, stating that "*Revenge* is very much a woman's film, especially in the first half. A powerful, obsessive story about forbidden love, it's what every woman dreams of, of being swept off her feet by someone who comes along."

The director added, "you can smell the energy, you can smell the vibrations between the two of them [Costner's and Stowe's characters.]"

Even after all the problems, Costner seemed to have a special feeling about this film. It did not make money and he was unhappy about its production problems, but he talks about it as if there were a certain camaraderie, regardless of the tension.

"I had to use my considerable weight at the box office to get the movie made," he said. "To me, it's like picking a football team. The story makes sense and it was obvious that I should play quarterback or end. I mean, Cochran is a role that I should have played."

What the critics said about

REVENGE

In NEWSWEEK (David Ansen)
The plot of *Revenge* is as lurid and basic as the title. Attractive ex-pilot (Kevin Costner) falls in love with the beautiful wife of his friend, a ruthless, powerful, aging Mexican millionaire (Anthony Quinn). Millionaire discovers the infidelity and takes revenge. Pilot is beaten to a pulp and left for dead. Wife has face slashed, is taken to a whorehouse and turned into heroin addict. Pilot recovers and sets out to find her. Much blood spills.... Costner gives a charismatic star performance but never abandons himself totally to the character.

In PEOPLE
"Costner and Madeleine Stowe paw each other with

convincing ardor, despite having to pay homage to that fixation of screenwriters, standing-up sex. As Costner wanders around with little happening, you start to notice how hazy a lot of scenes are for no apparent purpose. You realize that writers Jim Harrison and Jeffrey Fiskin, adapting Harrison's novella, give people stilted lines like, 'I can't see being a lapdog for some Mexican kingpin.'"

In NEW YORK
"Tony Scott's *Revenge* is about Mexico the way his brother Ridley Scott's *Black Rain* is about Japan. Scene after scene is given over to the glib, passive, voluptuous atmospherics of commercial photography.... Along with Ridley Scott and Adrian Lyne, Tony Scott is one of the former English commercial-makers who have practically destroyed American film aesthetics over the past ten years. These men shoot movies in the style of lingerie ads. Their technique of indiscriminate aural-visual 'mood' painting is the very opposite of drama. What, for instance, is the dramatic function of all that lace? *Revenge* may be sexy and violent, but it's also lethally boring, and the reason lays in the way Scott works.... The images are overlit and overcut, yet some of the actors manage to come through – or at least parts of them come through. I have a strong impression of Costner's awkward smile."

PART

3

THE MAN & THE FUTURE

CHAPTER

9

THE FAMILY MAN

Any celebrity who has a family often faces a difficult struggle in many ways. First, they must try to keep their family and their career separate from one another. In addition, they must find the time away from a busy and demanding career to spend time with the other most important things to them – their spouse and children.

Costner, due to the wonderful times he shared with his father as a young child, hopes he and Cindy can be similar types of parents – in spite of the Hollywood baggage. The Costners have three children: Annie, 6, Lilly, 4, and Joe, 2.

"Cindy and I talk a lot about raising those kids. I want them to like being with their family and doing things with us, like I did with my dad – hunting, fishing, together. I bring them to movie locations with Cindy. I keep them with me. I think about, 'What if I'm not around? What if the next plane I'm on to London doesn't make it?' I want them to have a dad they remember. What if I'm not around when they start learning how to drive, or not home to discipline them when they come in late? Or not home for dinner with them after work, like my dad always was? I've gotta be their parent. That's the most important thing," he says.

Costner is realistic enough to know that he cannot always guide his children, but he would like to be a strong enough presence to affect them until they reach adulthood. He regards his children as his most treasured possession.

"I'm not responsible for their behavior for the rest of their lives, but I have to be there for them now," he said. "To tell them when they please me and why. It isn't important who my kids are. What matters is the kind of people they become. I want to live to see that, at least until they're 18. I want to have been with them at least that far."

Trying to be a normal family with all the trappings,

stress and perks that come from major stardom is not an easily-accomplished goal. The Costners are well aware of this and work hard at doing just that. As Kevin sees it, "You're under intense scrutiny all the time" from the press.

"I try to protect my family from that," he added. "Cindy and I sure as hell aren't perfect. We don't have a perfect marriage by any means, but we work at it. People are surprised our marriage works. It seems they wish it didn't, because you're a star and so your marriage isn't supposed to work. I don't want to be known as a man who steals another guy's wife. I want to be like my dad, home with my kids at night. It can be rough."

Expecting to be like his dad is probably a goal set too high for Costner to realistically achieve. After all, he had the type of dad who was always home after work and who spends his time with the family on the weekend.

Although Costner doesn't mind not being as "perfect" a father as his own, he laments that people expect him to fail at it merely because of his celebrity status. "Why is it people seem to expect a movie star to fail?" he wonders. "They expect you to pay for your good luck – to see your marriage collapse or drugs destroy you or some terrible thing. Then it will be Kevin who had too much success too early, and now he's finally paying for it." What about the decade he did pay?

One drawback of Kevin's career has been his tempestuous love scenes and the fact that he is consider a sex symbol. This causes a great deal of problems with his wife, who finds herself working overtime to deal with the insecurities, disappointments and fears that go along with the territory when one's husband is a star. Cindy says she works all the time to be stronger than the pressures, and

Costner reveals he could not do as well as she.

"It's not easy for her," he shares. "If Cindy's and my roles were reversed, I don't think I could handle it. Now all the attention is on me... 'Kevin this, Kevin that.' What praise there is, whatever criticism is, is focused on me. Cindy's got to be incredibly strong to deal with all that. I want my family to live as normal a life as possible. I don't want my kids to think they're special because of me."

One reason the sex scenes can be difficult on all concerned is because few know how the scenes will look until the movie is finished. Costner explains it this way: "One problem is that [Cindy] doesn't know what to expect until she sees it on the screen. I don't explain to my wife what I'm going to do onscreen because I don't know what I'm going to do in every situation. For instance, in bed with Susan Sarandon, in *Bull Durham*, I improvised the painting of her toenails."

The problems connected with being a star are not the only thing that make it difficult for Costner to keep a balance between career and family. He finds that the excessive rewards which come from being a huge success have the potential to be as damaging to his children's future development than the problems – perhaps more so.

"I worry about the shadow I cast," he explained. "My children travel first-class. My children travel in a limousine. I didn't travel in a limousine until I was 28. And when it showed up at my house, I went out and took a *picture* of it. On some level, my children will probably never know that's really a privilege. They will have a lot of high-class problems. I want my children to think they're special, but I don't want them to think they're better than anybody else."

Aside from the inherent problems of having a parent

who is a "star," Costner confesses that he could work much harder at parenting. Lack of time seems to be his biggest enemy in doing so.

He harbors his guilty feelings over not being the type of father his dad was for him. "I know I can do better with relationships with my family, and I have to figure out how. There's just not enough time for the people I care about. I'm a good dad – when I'm at home. But when I'm away, my motel-room walls aren't lined with pictures of my family. Maybe something is wrong with me, but I separate things in order to keep exploring who I am. It's a high-class set of problems that cut into my creativity and my family life. I don't want to stop what I'm doing, and I don't want to lose what I have," he related.

Costner feels that a main source of the problem with keeping his children from having an "abnormal and unreal" perspective is that stars are often treated as royalty. They are not judged by what they have done or for who they are, but are merely labeled as such, clouding all the personal issues behind the person.

"I have the same problem with stardom that I have with royalty," Costner said. "They're judged not by the quality of their ideas but by their birthright. I didn't set out to be a star. If you do, you engage in manipulation. You do stuff to be liked. I didn't want to be endorsed; I wanted to be listened to. I had ideas about things."

Mr. Mom is a role that Kevin Costner was not born to play, although he does relate the story of how he had to take care of his first daughter when Cindy went back to school. Costner is not afraid to have his family come before his career, as evidenced by the fact that his children's needs must come before, or at least be equal to, his own.

"When Annie was born, Cindy went right back to school and I took care of her for the first two, three months. She was easy. She'd sleep from seven to seven and take two naps. We didn't realize how great she was until Lilly came along. She gets up whenever she wants and she's not regular at all. But they're both smilers. One day we brought Annie down to the sound stage where I was working. A bright light turned on behind Annie and Cindy and I was in costume and didn't want Annie to be afraid, so I called out, 'Hey, Annie!' And she kind of strutted across the stage and put her fingers across my lips and said, 'Quiet, Dad, they're making a movie here,'" he recalled.

Still, daddy Costner admits that the difficulties of trying to move forward in his career and raising a baby expressed to him the difficulties of being a working parent. He admits he doesn't know how single mothers who must work handle their duties. For him, "It was hard but I loved it. I took her on my meetings, sometimes some pretty high-level ones. I'd say, 'Can you turn your phones down a little bit?... They're waking up my kid.' And if Annie needed care, if her diaper needed changing – the meeting came to a halt."

All Costner's film contracts stipulate that he receive round-trip airfare for his wife and three children so that they may visit him while shooting on location. "I take less money [per movie]," he admits, "but it's worth it." The family visited him on location in England for Thanksgiving dinner during the making of *Robin Hood: Prince Of Thieves*.

When he's not taking them with him on location, Costner takes the kids hunting and fishing with him just like his father used to do. "My dad was always there for me and my brother, and I want my kids to have the same kind of dad – a dad they will know. Being a dad is the most important thing in my entire life," he emphasized.

Perhaps the Costner children will model their father's beliefs about Hollywood and his film career. If they do, they should end up as down to earth as the star sounds explaining that he is not "too cool" for all this.

"I don't want to make too much pretension about this business. I don't like to be too cool about it. I don't want to be too cool about the projects I do. There are lots of people out there who would like to be doing what I'm doing" he admits.

It is easy to see Costner's concern for his family and children from these statements. From the following one, it is also easy to see that he is devoted to his children and wants to be a role model for them: "The great thing about my daughter is that I was the first man ever to touch her. I was the first man to ever put my hands on her and from that day on she'll compare other men to me."

When push comes to shove and career matters take precedence, however, Costner is realistic about the fact that he tries as hard as he can to be a good father, and that sometimes he must honor his film commitments before his family ones.

"I take my kids to school, but I have work to do," Costner says. "Scenes don't happen by magic." One of the issues that has made it extremely difficult for Cindy and Kevin is the "stud" image that he portrays in most of his film roles. In response to this image, one can see the frustration Costner must at times feel from trying to reassure his wife it's *her* that he has the *real* love story with. "I don't think it's even a thing to discuss," he says defensively. "People need labels and they'll find them for me the way they find them for someone else. I'm not immune to the trappings of this business. But I don't go to it. I just think women respond to roles and it's all a cumulative effect from the movie. It's not just me."

Yet, for all his success, Costner can still do errands and chores with a minimum of hassle. He has to shop for groceries, take the cars to be repaired and chauffeur the children when Cindy is unable. He sounds like a feminist dream when he explains why he is willing to help out with raising the kids and household matters.

"People haven't started bothering me at the grocery, which is a good thing because I insist on going," he reports. "I don't want to become a recluse, and, with three kids, sometimes my wife can't go. So I have to help out."

Nonetheless, for those of us who would like to imagine Costner making goo-goo eyes and cooing to his children, it is not the "doting" image of father that he has of himself. As he tells it, "I love my children. I pay attention to them. I could talk about them for a long time. But I'm not the kind of father who, when my wife was pregnant, painted the nursery blue. I'm concerned about what they'll think about the world, and how they'll figure out how they fit into it. What they *do* won't be as important."

When asked if he would encourage his children to follow in his career footsteps, Costner seemed to take a liberal approach to the issue. He said, "I wouldn't fear for my children to do what I do, but I wouldn't encourage it, either. I'm more interested in what type of persons they will become."

It is encouraging to see a father who, at least in theory, says that he is more interested in what his children will *become* as opposed to what they shall *do*. As Abraham Lincoln said, "I am not interested in who my grandfather was. I am much more interested in who his grandson will be." Costner does resist at all costs the temptation to describe the cute behavior his children, like any children, can exhibit at their ages. When asked about the pressures of dealing with the press where his family's intimate moments are concerned, he responded, "Pressures? You have to do the best you can. As yet, the gossip writers haven't linked me with anyone. I know they will at a certain point and that will be hurtful. But by and large, the press has been good to me and I think that is because when I do talk, it's about the movies. When I did *The Untouchables* I didn't work for 10 or 11 months and I didn't talk. Sure, my kids do cute things. So what. So do yours, I bet. Who gives a fuck?"

Sometimes the press labels Costner and his wife, a former Snow White, "the perfect couple." Yet, Costner says anyone who believes that is making a very superficial reading of the whole matter and is quick to correct that erroneous image. "There's a misnomer here. It's real easy to be 'America's Couple.' He's married. They're gonna have three kids. He's doing leads in movies in America. He's getting X amount of dollars. She's not in the business. Isn't that great! Isn't that refreshing! If you paint it like that then... but we struggle like everyone else, and I don't want to dwell on it, but marriage is not an easy institution. It's difficult, and made more difficult by this industry. If anything did happen it would be assumed that "it got them," but that might not be the case. Nobody knows what we go through on a personal basis, from day to day, film to film, but we're trying like everyone else... This is about as deep as I ever get into it."

Costner gets angry when someone brings up his "ways" with the ladies. He does not like to see himself portrayed in this image, and when pressed about it, he can respond sarcastically and crudely, as he does here in response to a query about his sex-symbol image: "People say that all these women want to have sex with me, but that's bullshit. That's because of respect for what you've done rather than what you look like. If I'm so hot, then ring up for three girls! Tell them if they want me they've gotta deal with all three of us [there were three people present during the interview] and see how magnetic my appeal is. Hell, don't write that. Or if you do, then make it humorous."

It is not only the pressures on his family that can derail a celebrity, it is more often the "fast track" and sordid lifestyles associated with the movie capital of the world. Costner knows it is easy to succumb to the temptations if one does not constantly work against it and says that scene was never close to him anyway.

"It's very easy to get caught up in the Hollywood lifestyle – the parties, the drugs – but that's not me. And that's not what's good for my family. I like to go jogging and, most of all, I feel it's important to eat the right foods. I know this sounds wholesome as hell, but I'm still a real person. And my health and the health and well-being of my family will always come first."

Others close to the Costners recognize that their relationship must resist enormous pressures and is one that requires great effort and maturity. As Cindy's brother David Silva, an assistant director on *Dances With Wolves* observes of their relationship: "It's got its problems. But she can tell me with her eyes how things are. I know that it wasn't easy at the beginning. But I think she's grown with it real well. She's an amazing person. She's kind of a wedge. She fits into any situation."

Kevin's brother also praises Cindy as the glue in their marriage. "She's been a good wife to Kevin. It's got to be tough on the spouse. This business is such an emotional roller coaster. It's bigger than life and the stakes are high," he said.

Costner does not try to present himself as being "perfect," an image he detests. It's just that he is very self-assured about what he knows.

"I know everything I know," he said. "And I'm not trying to seem like a fucking good guy. Maybe I *am* a good guy. Huh? Ever think about that?"

Costner seems to find it easier to resist the Hollywood scene by retaining his common sense. The Costners didn't "chuck everything" and buy a mansion in Beverly Hills the minute Kevin made it. As he expresses, "Cindy and I aren't penny-pinchers, but we really hold onto things. Hell, it wasn't until three years ago that we finally got rid of the last bit of our college furniture. You feel insecure about giving things up because, who knows, you might need them some day."

This characteristic could also arise from Costner's upbringing and his father's Dust Bowl struggles, which gave him a firm sense of the value of a dollar. In addition, the memories of their early struggling years are more than likely still vivid in the mind of both Costners.

Still, the motivation behind his actions are not easy to gauge. Costner does not disclose a great deal of information about himself, and says ulterior motives are not very often found within him.

"People aren't aware of what makes me do what I do," he related. "I don't have a lot of motives. I have a lot of ambition. I don't know where the ambition comes from, but it's not motive-driven. It's the ability to be inspired, and knowing what that feeling is."

The Costners have four homes, including a pink hacienda in the hills above Pasadena, a four-bedroom condo in the High Sierras used for their hunting and fishing trips, their main home in La Canada and a beach house in Santa Barbara.

The two find it difficult to deal with the constant spotlight on Kevin. "He loves the attention he's getting from everybody. He loves people, and it doesn't matter to him if it's a man or a woman who's appreciating him," says a friend. "It's difficult, almost impossible, really, for Cindy, and she lets him know about it. She's a strong woman, and she's entitled to her feelings. It's a bone of contention between them all the time. But they love each other, the marriage is strong, and if it ever broke up, it's she who would have to do it."

The Costners' friend, author Michael Blake, is also aware of the stress their relationship has experienced as a result of Kevin's career. He has hope for them and faith in their relationship, however, especially in light of what they've gone through and the fact that they've still retained their love and respect for each other.

"They've already weathered a hell of a lot," says Michael Blake, the screenwriter of *Dances With Wolves*. "Just the fact that they're still together says a lot about their union. Kevin is extremely conservative, and he doesn't believe in breaking up, no matter what."

When the problems start to pile up, Cindy and Kevin work on trying to solve them. They have to be quite mature to handle this as the enormous pressure can often cause tempers to flare and impatience to hold court of reason and tolerance. "I guess it's a certain amount of maturity that tells you when things are going bad, they're not going to get better because you make a change, that your life won't transform magically," he said. "And ultimately, the only thing you have in your life is your family."

Additionally, "the sex symbol hook is flattering, but it makes me the prime target of gossip," says the star. Uneasy with his sex symbol image, Costner nevertheless admits to enjoying it away from the press.

"I've been involved in scenes in bathtubs and bedrooms and on kitchen tables, but I never even feel comfortable when I have to take my shirt off. [After] that scene in *Wolves* where I was naked – that was in the book, to show his vulnerability and how comfortable he felt being alone – I found the biggest reeds I could hide behind," Costner laughs.

"What turns me on is not graphic sex, but the potential for romance," he added. "The tension between wanting to do something – and not doing it. The thing that makes us go, man... To undress somebody? It's the coolest thing. To be undressed. To be touched. To be physically, somehow just taken... "

In *No Way Out*, the sex scenes with Sean Young were so passionately involved that there was trouble on the homefront. Costner worried in advance there might be, knowing he had to share the back seat of a limousine with Sean Young. He did so very nervously reports his co-star.

"I think Kevin's got a deep puritanical strain in him, oh, positively," says Young. "It was a very difficult scene to do. I was the vulnerable one, because I was naked and I don't really enjoy being naked. So I had told a lot of jokes. I kept a poll of how many cast and crew members had screwed in cars. I had never screwed in a car. Just about everybody else had except me. It's just not my bag."

Costner, who has said publicly that he can appreciate beautiful women, defends his scene with Young.

"Look, we're all redblooded dudes. Someone takes her clothes off, I mean, there comes a point where you have to look. But we had to be real hungry and Sean understood that. But I had no feeling whether it was intense at all" Costner added.

One wonders whether Cindy understood the backseat "hunger" and if she can accept his belief that there is "no feeling" to it. For the Costners' sake, one hopes both Cindy and Kevin will continue to understand for another 13 years.

CHAPTER

10

KEVIN COSTNER: THE MAN

The struggling young actor who collected Coke bottles to buy lunch is now a multimillionaire whose price goes up every time he says "no."

Although Costner enjoys his newfound wealth, it truly hasn't changed his tastes as much as one might assume. Kevin drives a Shelby Mustang and a Bronco instead of the Porsche, Mercedes or Ferrari favored by lesser known celebrities.

He and his wife still enjoy taking their kids camping with them and doing the same activities that Costner enjoyed with his mother and father when they were too poor to afford any other type of vacation.

Most actors of Costner's standing would have on the wall a Matisse or Picasso, but Costner plans to hang the canoe he built before entering college on the walls of his home.

Costner despises the "formal dining process," as he calls it, insisting he is the type that "likes to mop up the gravy with bread."

"When I go out, my pits start to sweat when I can't figure out what's on the menu. I just order what the guy on the left does," he says. He'd rather have a draft beer than a martini and he has a passion for Hostess Twinkies.

Claiming that he would enjoy a lifestyle far removed from the Hollywood scene, maybe even mining for gold in the Klondike, he says: "I've always gone for the biggest adventure. I've always wanted a story."

The only concession to his newfound riches? He bought his parents a red Silverado for Christmas a few years back so they could travel around the country in their recreational vehicle. As he stated, "It had to be a Silverado pick-up."

Is Costner a man happy with his current lifestyle and all

the pressures that come from trying to maintain a family and mega-sized career? "Hell, yes!" he exclaims in his best Jake (his "Silverado" character) enthusiasm.

"You'd be a fool not to be. It doesn't mean I don't have frustration and insecurities. For one thing, I wish I were smart. You know that *Big Chill* crowd [of actors]? Those guys are really smart, really clever. I'm a bit of a bumpkin. No, really. But I have a piece of ground that I hold, and I won't be intimidated."

The "piece of ground" he holds onto with the tenacity and determination of a pitbull dog is also what makes it difficult for co-workers to deal with when he won't back down from an issue. Still, Costner admits that most of his success is based on the gift of instinct.

He mourns the fact that there was not enough discipline in his nature to be better educated in real terms. As he admits, "I wish I was more disciplined. I wish I had dedicated myself more to my studies and I wish I was better read. I read all the time, and then I think of all the books that I won't have time to read before I die, and it frustrates me. And, like a kid, I still need to be liked, to please. I need validation. If it's a weakness, I choose to keep it."

This sense of needing validation could be the element which keeps Costner a little bit down-to-earth now that he has become a huge success. Surely during his early struggling phase he kept more to himself and his family. His career was the focus and he was determined enough to make it that it took up all his energy.

Now, 15 pounds overweight, with a reputation for being the latest Hollywood "Frankenstein" and with a career in full bloom, Costner seems to be forgetting his priorities and values. This is not be the first time an "innocent" and "good" guy fell prey to the temptations and pressures of the film business. If Costner's priorities and values were still as firmly rooted within him as when he wanted to make it as opposed to "being a success," he might not be having as many personal problems.

Take for instance, his complete alienation of long-time friend and director Kevin Reynolds. Reynolds, who basically gave Costner his professional start in *Fandango*, traveled to the *Dances With Wolves* set to lend moral and technical support to director Costner, even filming scenes in that movie that made it to the screen.

As a favor to him, Costner chose to do Reynolds' next film, Morgan Creek Production's *Prince Of Thieves*. However, by that time Costner was an Oscar-winning director and producer and he seemed to forget his boundaries as an actor.

He reportedly bickered constantly with Reynolds over every shot and even seized the camera at one point and filmed a partial scene. The two argued so much that each was drained by the time the filming was completed. Each has vowed to never work with the other and the final battle had Costner siding with executives against his long-time friend and director.

Reynolds will only say of the experience that "the pressures eventually become very draining." Costner was also cautious, saying, "There was not a lot of patience on the set." Each felt the film to be their least satisfying artistic endeavor and their friendship for now remains strained at best.

Tenacious, stubborn and intense, Costner has long been known since his first minor role in *Frances* to be a proverbial pain in the ass. Many agree that his perfectionism is admirable from a distance, but few have not expressed their relief when Costner's questions and nit-picking finally end after a role is completed.

Even good friend Lawrence Kasdan had to use his brother as a go-between when working with Costner due to his incessant attention to detail. One would think that Costner would think these things out or question his character's motivations and actions long before arriving on the set. He should at least realize that if he is insecure about the type of performance he may be giving, his questions and ideas should be limited. After all, a director has more than one actor's performance to worry about and devoting his time exclusively to one person's performance could help diminish the overall impact of the film.

You'd think that as director, Costner would understand that making things difficult during shooting can only add to the costs of a film and extend the time it takes to make it. Perhaps this incessant questioning concerning his characters' roles and motivation stems from a profound insecurity as to whether or not he is going to give a solid performance.

On the other hand, maybe a man who professes to a lack of intelligence and a plodding nature really *needs* all the extra attention and questioning to understand.

"I'm not that smart a person to begin with," Costner lamented, "not that forward a thinker. I'm not that well-read and just basic in the I.Q. things. I didn't score that well. I have instincts for things and a great love for film. In other things, I'm really not that clever or advanced."

Great instincts and a love of film have been possessed by nearly every great Hollywood talent. As Costner's career grows and the pressures become more intense, his apparent lack of intelligence could prove a detriment. Determination and perseverance may have taken Costner to the heights he has scaled thus far, but that lofty seat can be difficult to maintain.

His future decisions and on-the-set behavior will more than likely determine the fate of his career and his personal happiness. Costner would be wise to become less insistent about having everything his own way. Should he make a wrong career or personal move at this point in his career, it may be too late before he realizes he has done irreparable damage to his reputation or image. Take the Sheri Stewart affair, for example. Does a Hollywood superstar with three lovely children and a beautiful and devoted wife truly have such longing and unfulfillment inside that he must apparently seek outside companionship?

A man who is more little boy than adult has got to realize that some of the behaviors that looked rakish and charming on him in his twenties, now, at nearly. 40, look more like irresponsibility and superficiality.

Writer Barbara Lippert has said that "Costner still projects an earnestness that's entirely devoid of irony." However, she also went on to say very astutely that "in the era of the condom earring, any screen icon worth his salt stands for fatherhood, monogamy and saving the environment."

But monogamy seems to be a thing of the past where Costner's "goody two shoes" image is concerned. Perhaps the "salt" Lippert refers to should be sprinkled by Cindy Costner on her husband's tail. He seems to have forgotten, temporarily at least, where his heart lay.

Amazingly, and perhaps due to that "lack of intelligence," Costner doesn't seem to realize that he has placed himself under a microscope where public and media scrutiny are concerned, which is one reason he makes millions of dollars yearly. As a result, he should be careful and remember the overnight destruction of reputations that infidelities caused in the lives of Gary Hart and Donald Trump. It might not be so bad if Costner's actions didn't go directly against the image he has tried to construct for over a decade. As Lippert also noted, "Clearly, what makes Kevin Costner perfect husband material for the Bush era is that he comes across as a focused, caring family man, a *provider* who's even got that vision thing." He should use that vision to wise up, and protect what is most valuable to him by resisting the temptations of more sordid things.

Other than weakness, why would a man risk losing something he had to work so hard and for so many years to build? Costner should also, since he cares so much about them, be fully aware of the messages this type of behavior is sending out to his children and fans. In the era of AIDS, it is sad to see that he would apparently be the carrier of the message that it's okay to screw around.

Costner's reported behavior is unfair to his wife and children and is one more sign that his selfish and vain behavior does exist. To please himself, at *any* cost, seems to be his motto. He should remember that if the cost is his personal life, his happiness and maybe even his career, it might not be worth indulging in "instant gratification." Too many great men have ruined their entire lives by being unable to resist "instant gratification" versus "long-term reward."

Costner's alleged dalliances may just be the straw that breaks his long-suffering wife's back. After putting up with all the years of struggle, all the tempestuous love scenes onscreen and her constant efforts to remain in the shadow of her husband's spotlight, Cindy Costner's patience may be wearing thin. She is a strong woman, friends assert, and it is likely she will not stand by and let her husband trash the immense amount of care and effort that has gone into their 13-year marriage.

Although Lippert had no conclusive proof that Costner had been unfaithful, revelations of an affair with Sheri Stewart have come to light, along with reports that the marriage has shown strains since the birth of their third child. The *Village Voice* in April of 1991 was slightly more insightful, saying only that "maybe Costner cheats on his wife." "I know someone who says she slept with him," an anonymous source disclosed.

As the star says, perhaps in partial defense to temptations of the flesh: "I always get a lot from what people say. I get juiced by people. But if you knew how harmful it could be at home, just some 'bull' story, whether true or not... there is just a lot of speculation."

Speculation or not, others have labeled it more harshly. In February, 1991, while shooting *Robin Hood: Prince Of Thieves*, Costner allegedly slept with a nightclub hostess named Sheri Stewart. For months after the *Thieves* shoot, just prior to Christmas of that year, no one was aware of just how well Costner was earning his sex symbol image.

The anonymity of the *Village Voice* article was not to be Costner's for long. In the February Fleet Street tabloids, Sheri Stewart revealed in near full detail, the steamy and passionate sexual encounters she shared with Kevin Costner. The affair consisted of a series of encounters while the filming of *Thieves* occurred.

What is most disturbing about the revelations of Costner's behavior is that the affair was going on at the same time that his wife and children flew to London to be with him for Thanksgiving. Apparently, Costner was the real turkey at the annual celebration. Headlines screamed from the front page as the Hollywood's "good guy" got caught with his pants down: "Costner Was *Wolf* In My Bed," "Costner Picks A Lover That Looks Like The Missus," and "Why I Picked Up Sluts By Costner."

The revelations in the article were shocking. Stewart's description of the night reads like a love scene from one of Costner's films. Stewart, 27, said she met Costner at a London nightclub known as Stringfellows. She admits that Costner asked her to go back to his hotel. When he entered the room, he was "carrying a bottle of wine and two glasses," she reported.

Costner's boyish enthusiasm seems as much an element in his sexual escapades as exists in his career. Stewart says, "He told me, 'I'm so excited you're here!' He was bouncing up and down like a little boy." Costner was staying at a posh West London hotel, but the reported object of his desire says "the only room I saw that night was the bedroom."

She says he took her directly to the bedroom. They sat on a bed and chatted for a while (perhaps Costner was not fooling when he said he could "talk to sluts" in his youth easier than other types of women. Another Fleet Street paper reported Costner as saying, "I can talk to sluts, and I don't use that term badly.")

After a while, Costner allegedly leaned over and kissed her and "one thing led to another," as she reported. However, the image she gives of Costner as a lover seems to have nothing to do with the man who is supposedly embarrassed by his sex symbol image and his onscreen love scenes.

"He was so passionate he brought tears to my eyes," she

recalls. She describes Costner as a carefree bachelor just come to town and that, she was a "grown woman, and the chemistry was just right."

Stewart went on to reveal even more of their intimate encounter. "I was wearing a flowing white dress. He had that off in no time. Underneath, I was wearing a sexy little teddy. He was so full of passion that if he would have had his way, he would have ripped the dress off, and the teddy right off my body."

Stewart, a former diving champion, admits that Costner truly satisfied her. "He really made me feel like a woman. He kept asking me, 'What can I do for you?' and 'How can I please you?'" This was not the end of it. As is straight out of his love scene with Susan Sarandon in *Bull Durham*, Costner was sexy and romantic. Stewart goes on to say that the encounter "made me feel incredibly sexy. He was doing charming things like kissing my feet and nuzzling my legs. It was such an incredible turn on."

After an early morning rendezvous, Stewart recalled falling asleep in his arms. She awoke at 8 a.m., only to find Costner hovering over her. "Shhh, don't make a sound," he reportedly told her. "My business associates are about to arrive."

Although Stewart said she would gladly leave, he apparently told her, "Just close all the connecting doors to the bedroom." Exhausted from her night of passion, Stewart fell asleep and reportedly awoke to Costner's climbing back into bed with her to "take up where he had left off."

Stewart's account is particularly startling considering Costner's image and the devotion his wife has shown him through 13 years of struggle and success. Moreover, Stewart claims the affair did not end with their nearly all-night love session. About 10 days later, Costner had reportedly relocated to another hotel, registered under the assumed name Alva Marshall, then called her just after midnight one evening, telling her to "come on over."

This time, Stewart was startled at the opulence and sumptuous furnishings in Costner's suite. "It was the biggest bed I've ever seen," she commented. Again, there wasn't a whole lot of preliminary chatter. "We went straight to bed. I realized this was only going to be a physical relationship, but I thought, 'What the hell?' This is a gorgeous guy, so why should I care?"

True to his words about the thrill of undressing someone and "touching," Stewart confessed she was wearing cowboy boots and jeans and that Costner really "got off on watching me undress." Stewart, 27, is ten years younger than Costner and looks amazingly like Costner's wife Cindy. Sheri recalls being surprised over her first glimpse of Mrs. Costner.

"When I saw her for the first time, it was just like looking in the mirror. All the time he was *making* love to me, he was probably *thinking* of her," she surmises. However, she says that Costner "never mentioned his family, but I knew he was married." She does reveal that "he didn't act like a married man with me."

After their second alleged night of lovemaking, Costner invited Stewart to a private screening of *Dances With Wolves*. An amusing note of interest is that Stewart felt herself getting jealous over Costner's passionate love scenes in the movie.

"The strangest moment," she says, "was when he made love on screen. It's a very passionate scene and I was looking at them and then looking over at him watching it. I found myself getting jealous."

Stewart's last encounter with the star came right before Christmas. They went to a restaurant where reservations were made under the name John Dunbar (Lt. Dunbar was the *Dances With Wolves* character). "He was pleased to see me," Stewart reported, "but it was different between us that night. He was the delightful lover he had been, but there was an underlying tension. I remember joking that I hoped we could always be friends, and he said, 'Well, we certainly won't be pen pals.'" Perhaps this underlying tension arose as a result of Costner, the family man, realizing what he was doing to his family – especially at Christmas time.

Costner returned home soon after and some time later, Stewart reported that she received a telephone call from a friend of his. The friend said, "Kevin is worried that people might find out about you," and Stewart said she "gathered it was over." She reports being really "spooked" when she saw Costner's wife and believes Costner's passion was really little more than type-casting in retrospect.

"I thought he chose me because I remind him of her. I was selected to play a role. I was charmed into co-starring in Kevin's sexual fantasies. I've heard of playing an actress's double on the set, but I never expected to find I had played Kevin's wife in real life," she said.

At one point earlier in his career, Costner tried to explain the feelings he has about such earthly temptations. "So you start talking to somebody and find them incredibly interesting. They happen to wear a skirt and are very beautiful and attractive to you and you can't stop being attracted to people and you can't stop being around them to see what they have to offer." Some believe Costner might mean he *doesn't* want to stop being attracted to others or being around them. However, with the high stakes he is risking (his career image, his wife's love and the stability of his family), one would think Costner could find the will power to resist soiling his character.

Another little-known aspect of Kevin Costner's life is that he is the lead singer and guitarist in a legitimate rock group called "Roving Boy." The group has been together for approximately seven years and consists of Costner and a three-member instrumental group: Blair Forward, Steve Appel and John Coinman. The group's first album was released in Japan. It was a ten-song compilation entitled "The Simple Truth" and was distributed outside North America with a heavy emphasis on the Japan market.

Costner has confined his singing debut to overseas markets, as do many celebrities when they make television commercials that they wouldn't be caught dead having aired in the states. For example, Paul Newman (a Costner favorite) has made a coffee commercial in Japan, while Woody Allen pushed a department store and Francis Coppola pitches whiskey. A unit of Tokuma Japan, a subsidiary of the giant Tokuma Group, pressed the platter to coincide with their first U.S. office, which opened in Los Angeles in 1988 (an event Costner attended).

About his private second career, Costner said, "I don't tell people all the things I do. Music is very private to me. I have to very careful how it's handled." A little confusion surrounded exactly how the album's title cut was going to be used in Japan. The chairman and chief executive of Tokuma, Yasuyoshi Tokuma, reported that "the song was played as the 'theme song' on the soundtrack of 'Dun-Huang,'" a $35-million period-drama that the Tokuma group co-produced last year with the Chinese government. The tune was used in the film and to promote it, but it did not make it on the soundtrack to "Dun-Huang."

The film was not a commercial success, and there are those that say the reason Costner's album is not available in the U.S. is because it's a "stinker." In other words, there is no one who feels that Costner should give up his acting career to become a rock and roll singer.

The single did go to Number 1 on Japan's foreign record chart, but it has only sold 13,000 copies since its April 25, 1988, release. It is only ranked 67 on the domestic pop chart in Japan. An LP with the same name as the single was released in July of that year and has sold 10,000 copies to date.

Chiharu Arifuku, the account manager at the record's sales agency said these figures are "pretty good" for a foreign group, but he added that the single is an "image song" for "Dun-Huang" more than a pop hit. Still, it would behoove the profit-oriented Japanese to realize a hit single *before* a film is opened is one way of generating audience interest and possibly increasing attendance.

In addition, the song had absolutely zero to do with the movie. The saga of romance and warfare set in 11-Century China begins *after* the "Roving Boy" single is released. The song can also be heard playing in the Japanese TV spot for Suntory malt beer. Costner's American representatives admit, though, that their star has "no plans for a U.S. recording career."

The actor admitted he recorded for Japan only because "that is what I felt most comfortable with. My singing and recording career have not been a long-time dream, rather a long-time pursuit." Robert Hillburn, noted *Los Angeles Times* record critic, was asked by his editor to review "The Simple

Truth" album. Said he: "Let's put it this way: if Costner were starring in a musical where it was crucial to the plot that the audience believe he's a really good singer, the producers would have to think about dubbing his voice. If recent albums by Don Johnson and Bruce Willis represented the 'good' and the 'bad' in celebrity pop performances, it's not stretching things too far to say that Costner's album represents the 'ugly.'"

Hillburn went on to say that Costner's problem, aside from an obviously complete lack of musical talent, is that he takes himself too seriously as a singer and composer for someone who doesn't have the necessary skill. Taking his film career seriously has always paid off for Costner, but musical risks apparently do not.

As Hillburn continues, this approach was totally wrong for his first album attempt: "It's not that he just shows little ability in the technical areas of singing, but he also demonstrates almost no hint of vocal character. Willis at least had the good sense to do playful remakes of R&B classics, whereas Costner takes himself seriously with original material [he wrote two cuts]. Anyway, even if Costner had given a performance on the level of Bruce Willis, it wouldn't be saying much."

This stinging review by the much-respected Hillburn may put a damper on one of Costner's pet film projects for the future – a remake of *Camelot*. "I really have a desire to play Arthur in *Camelot*," he says. "He is a very cool guy, and I think he's faced with a dilemma. He's losing his woman, his best friend, he's by himself and he starts talking to Merlin. He realizes in his babbling and trying to reconstruct his life that's he's stumbled onto his future – which some of us never do. There's that great feeling he has that he can rest easy because he'd done the right thing in his life. He's stumbled onto his destiny. That's kind of what I really wanted in my life, to stumble into my destiny head first, or back into it."

Anyway, Costner's seriousness is best reserved for film-making. To this end, his work space is atypical of most film stars. It is no-frills all the way. The major art on the weathered barnboard walls of his office is a flury of 3 x 5" cards that describe, one sentence per card, the plot of his next film.

Costner privately acknowledges how the Hollywood system has benefited him, but he also attacks it for the way it's weakened almost all of his films. He also admits to the pain of fan reactions when they are coarse and inconsiderate. "Sometimes I'll go to a party and I'll walk by a couple who don't know me and hear the woman say to her boyfriend, 'You're much more handsome than he is.' And that *hurts*. Look, the camera is real kind to me. I don't think of myself as classically good-looking. I know that when I walk into a roomful of guys, I'll come in fifth. Well, maybe fourth."

For the most part, Costner, the man, wears his traditional uniform of faded Levi 501 jeans, white T-shirts and cowboy boots. If he has to dress up in a suit he feels as uncomfortable, and looks it, as a reluctant 12-year-old on his way to Sunday school. He likes horses, guns, bows and arrows and he likes to jump from second-story buildings. He is also described as self-absorbed, vain and with a need to be the center of attention.

To this end, he remembers his mother scolding him, "Kevin, what's all this 'I' business?" Costner muses for a while that he might be more "one of us" these days.

"One of us, one of us," he says. "I actually kind of like

that. I don't like a lot of posturing. I don't like a lot of intrigue. It's tiring and it's hurtful. If I wanted someone to say something, that's kind of an interesting thing. It's not very eccentric, it's pretty even-Steven down the road. I guess maybe that's my deal."

Still, there can be no denying that success as much as Costner has experienced it can cost dearly. He barely tolerates the invasion of privacy that has become hidden underneath the word the 'press.'

"I get a sickening feeling when someone comes up to me and says, 'I read something about you.' My pits start to sweat when somebody says (that). Why do I have to go through that? I like what I do, but it's too bad I get all the money I get for it and it's too bad everybody has to write about it. It's too bad people have to pan it or give it endorsements. It's too bad we depend on that. Besides, I don't feel I have that much insight or am ultimately that interesting. I'm not the smartest guy you ever met, certainly not as smart as a lot people who've come to talk to me."

It's good to hear Costner admit the lucrative position he's in – it could be one reason why he must "put up with it." Another reason he might consider is that if he stops being an infidel and gets back to concentrating on his career, he may be earning himself a piece of immortality from his celluloid performances, which will remain intact long after Kevin Costner has. To cheat death by leaving a piece of you behind is a fairly big accomplishment. It seems at times Costner wishes it could be his without the downside.

In spite of the allegations of his recent affair, Costner says, "I have high survival instincts. I can see something coming, feel the temperature, see movements, shifts in people. Those feelers are always out." Yet after a 15-year career in one of the most competitive and ruthless industries in the world, Costner doesn't push his luck with those instincts any more: "I've tried in my life to tone down that survival instinct of thinking I know people. Because I'm pretty good at it. And the better you are, you suddenly start thinking, 'I know people'... and just about that time, you get it fucking wrong."

Trust and thinking he knows it all have come back to haunt Costner so often that he refuses to believe anything these days without proof. "I thought all my movies would be great. And they should have been great. Every one of them. And they weren't all great." Due to this, he is wary of trusting anyone but himself with the final cut of his films.

Costner feels bitter about all the money he's seen wasted in today's Hollywood. "Actors are not often appreciated by filmmakers and the reason is money. I'm very conscious of money when I do a scene, and there's probably hundreds of thousands of dollars in overspending that really doesn't have to do with the movie. I think movies are out of hand, moneywise. Crews are bloated. The crew may take hours to adjust a camera, but God forbid an actor needs a few minutes on the set to get himself into the right frame of mind. I find humans are infinitely more complicated than that F-stop." Costner is not alone in thinking Hollywood has gotten out of hand, business-wise. Jeffrey Katzenberg astounded Hollywood with last year's 35-page plus memo published in *Variety* blasting Hollywood for its insane and ever-escalating production costs. The memo stood as a reminder to the Disney filmmakers to get "back to basics." Peter Dekom, the powerful entertainment lawyer, also penned a memo to *Variety* admonishing the town to "cut costs" before cutting the very noses off their own faces because of the enormous budgets that fail to bring in their costs at the box office.

Costner feels it is also important to focus on a good script, but feels it is easier to pick a good play than a good script. "You take a play and throw it down and say, 'This isn't funny.' With a movie script it hasn't been done yet, and you have to be up to it. The challenge is not to play *smaller*, not to play *under* it. That's why I love Peter O'Toole. Everybody wants to start mumbling, be very breathy, moody, instead of being *out* there. O'Toole is the only guy who can be as big onstage as onscreen. He's somehow found a believable balance. He's naked. "

As to other roles in his future, Costner reaffirms the story as being the most crucial element to him. "I'm looking for roles of a lifetime. I put a lot of weight on picking the right movies. I need to do less of that. I sit and think about career decisions a little too much. Because I know people who do junk movies all the time and the next thing you know, they're in another good movie. Young actors, old actors, whatever. And it doesn't seem to affect them. I don't want to emulate them, but I'm always wondering, 'Why the hell am I so worried about things all the time? I worry about not being great. It bothers me if I'm not going to be really good."

One reason for Costner's powerful Hollywood image (he was ranked No. 13 in this year's *Premiere* ranking of the 100 most powerful people in Hollywood, being outranked by his own agent, Michael Ovitz, who came in at No. 1), is that the industry has not yet fully figured out just who Kevin Costner, the man, is.

Actor James Earl Jones, his co-star in *Field Of Dreams*, analyzes Costner's unique power in a town not known for allowing too much power. "Everyone wants power in this business," said Jones. "And Kevin's is a unique brand of power. It's not predictable. He's not after megamillions or making sure his ego is fulfilled. He isn't macho; he's pure male. If you press the wrong buttons, the man is dangerous. He won't explode – that's counterproductive – but he will set you straight right away. He's got away with things that a lot of up-and-comers couldn't have." How long will a system that prides itself on stripping power away from "too powerful" individuals let this go on? "Hard to say," says Jones. "It has to figure him out first."

Costner confirmed that the Hollywood scene and he do not mix well. "If you say what you mean in this town, you're an outlaw. You know you're on the right track if Hollywood finds you an enigma. People look at me and think they see everything. But what they see is one moment frozen in time. I've come from somewhere to get to that point. There's stuff in my back pockets, up my sleeve that they don't know anything about. I don't offer up everything there is, onscreen or in life. It's not guile. But conversation is supposed to be a two-way thing, and generally people want to know more about me than they want to reveal about themselves. So of course, I hold back. I'm not dying to tell people my story," he explained.

For a final word about Kevin Costner, the man, I let the actor speak for himself: "I consider myself a work in progress, even at this stage. I'm not even close to where I want to be. I'm just shit. I'm average. When I see someone do great work, I get terrified that I wouldn't do it that way. It drives me crazy. I like to have a lot of fun. I think there's a lot of larceny in me. If somebody feels like going, I'll go. I like forward motion. I believe in myself. I do things my way.

If acting ever stopped satisfying me, I would walk away. I would probably end up in the Pacific Northwest. I'm at peace up there. In many ways I was always a loner. I still am."

CHAPTER

11

JFK, THE BODYGUARD

& THE FUTURE

In Oliver Stone's upcoming *JFK*, Kevin Costner plays New Orleans District Attorney Jim Garrison, who tried to prove that New Orleans businessman Clay Shaw was part of a conspiracy to assassinate President John F. Kennedy. The prosecution attempt was unsuccessful and Garrison became a *persona non gratis* everywhere he went. However, Stone has uncovered some revealing information that sheds light on a possible CIA/FBI conspiracy. The movie is meeting with tons of controversy from just about everyone who has an interest in it. The film has already set off a fierce battle between the Oscar-winning director and George Lardner, a *Washington Post* reporter who thinks the screenplay is false and misleading. Costner is doing his best to stay out of the controversy surrounding the film, but once it is released at Christmas, he may no longer be able to do so.

The film, Costner's second for Warner Brothers, also stars Tommy Lee Jones, Sissy Spacek (reuniting the *Coal Miner's Daughter* co-stars) and Gary Oldman. Jack Lemmon, John Candy, Glenn Ford and Sally Kirkland make cameo appearances in the picture. According to one inside report, "there are over 200 speaking parts" in the $40-million film.

Garrison was the only one to conduct a criminal investigation of the assassination. He tried to prove through evidence that Kennedy was definitely the victim of a conspiracy and that Lee Harvey Oswald was set up as the fall guy.

Stone takes up the fight as he sets out to prove that the CIA and FBI were definitely connected to the conspiracy. Tommy Lee Jones plays International Trade Mart Director Clay Shaw, the man Garrison tried to prosecute for his involvement in the assassination plot. Shaw was acquitted, however, and Garrison's image became a little blackened by reports that he was trying to "frame" Shaw.

Costner has quite a metaphysical approach to acting. He believes that taking naps in between scenes allows him to dream about the character and stay "in character" as a result.

In a somewhat metaphysical description that would have method actors running for their Strausberg text, Costner reveals his acting secret: "I think a good deal about the character. Then I take a nap and actually have useable images come to me that I can use in the character. When making a movie, I don't generally hang around anybody on the set. I usually do the same thing. I'm the kind of guy who likes to get letters but doesn't like to write. I like to be with people, but I don't have to be. I don't know what that makes me. I don't spend a lot of time with the fringe benefits of my business. I'm not at Steamboat Springs or Celebrity Skiing."

Costner has always been self-sufficient and a bit of a loner. When he was a teenager, he hitchhiked across country and used to work on fishing boats as a cook. Still, it cannot be too uncommon to enjoy getting letters without having to return any.

Costner's *JFK* location visit had so many so thrilled to have a movie star in town that a "Kevin Watch" column was begum in which people write in about their experiences. One resident wrote:

"I was working at Sun Gear in the West End and it was a slow day, hardly anyone in the mall. It was around three o'clock Tuesday afternoon. He came in, and I thought to myself, 'Oh, he looks so familiar.'"

Wearing faded denim jeans with a pastel yellow polo T-shirt and his hair slicked back into a kind of wet look, Costner was reportedly accompanied by a young woman of about 20. She attractive and similarly attired.

"I kept thinking to myself, 'He looks so familiar,'" wrote the correspondent. "I knew something was up when he started saying, 'I'll take that one and that one and that one.' I was like, 'Wow, are you sure you want all of these sunglasses?' And he said, 'Yes, I'll take them.'

"And he started looking at other sunglasses and these two teenagers came up to me and said, 'Did he touch these sunglasses?' And I said, 'Yeah, why?' And they said, 'He's Kevin Costner!' And I went, 'Oh, my God, really?' From then on, I was so nervous, but he was real mannerly until all these people started coming into our store asking for autographs.

"Then he started telling me to kind of hurry it up. He charged $450 of merchandise on his gold American Express card. And I was like, 'Oh, I'm touching his card.' He signed all the autographs, 'Dances With Wolves, Kevin.' But mine he signed, 'To Cindy, see you at the movies. Love, Kevin.' Then he left." One can see from such a detailed report why celebrity-hood can sometimes become a burden, especially in public.

As filming began, it soon became known throughout New Orleans that Costner and crew would need lodging while filming *JFK* there. As Costner looked for a place with four bedrooms, four baths and a swimming pool for the bargain price of $7,000 per month, all types of bizarre offers started pouring in. One man offered his 52-room mansion, saying it was good because it was located on the "fashionable" St. Charles Avenue and was also used by Cable News Network during their coverage of the 1988 Republican National Convention. Another woman offered her home which only had three bathrooms but threw in the use of her Rolls Royce as an extra incentive.

On the low end of the scale came an offer from a man with a \$400-per-month efficiency unit. "I know it's too small for Costner and his family, but you never know," said the owner, reasoning that "someone else in the cast or crew may need a place to stay." Indeed, you never know.

In Dallas, where the filming resumed after New Orleans location work, the public reaction was equally strong about having a real "movie star" in town. The *Dallas Morning News'* "Kevin Watch" column helped encourage the throngs of miniskirted young women hoping to catch a glimpse of the sex symbol. Many wore miniskirts and beehive hairdos, hoping to be used in the film as extras. An open casting call for "60s" extras brought a response from more than 11,000 in their best "Camelot-era" garb as busy Interstate 30 was shut down for the filming and people were so excited by his presence they suggested Costner should actually think about running for mayor. Carol Luker, a bank vice president, and her three female friends spent one entire lunch break staring at the beige trailer which is Costner's dressing room. Their waiting finally paid off when they caught a glimpse of their favorite actor. Earlier, they'd been watching from the 66th floor of their office building.

"We all have our binoculars," Ms. Luker reported. "I'd say from all the women looking out the windows the whole building is leaning over to one side."

Still, there are those who report that Costner does not waste a second he does not have to on the set, especially when he is directing. He is meticulous about set dressing and prop arranging. As he notes these days (sometimes sounding a little arrogant, even spoiled by his success), "I'm at the real pain-in-the-ass point in my career where everything matters a lot. I have a very strong point of view about films. I don't think there is a point I can't make in movies. I'd like the kinds of movies I do to be benchmarks for their genre. That's my goal for the next ten years. What's the point of doing something if it's not original? As an actor, I'm a storyteller. My motives are about being an emotional detective in roles. But I find people here don't believe at the end of the day what they believed at the beginning. They all want to take a chance but, when they have to, they don't. I don't change my mind about stuff."

Acting well used to be Costner's chief concern. These days he is also obsessed with the story, plot, writing, editing, direction and other characters. Costner seems to be spreading his talents a little thin. He would be wise to remind himself of Michaelangelo's belief that "as every nation divided falls, so every mind divided among too many studies confuses and saps itself." Of course, this is the man who said before he directed his first film the smash *Dances With Wolves*), "I'm not anxious to show that I can direct just to prove something. When I direct, I want to direct a home run. You've got to want to do it because you believe in your story. People don't direct for the power. They go in for the completion of something they want to see. I don't want to be jacking off. I want to be where the light is."

Yet Costner seems a little disinterested in it now that he thinks he has it all. "I'm bored talking about that Hollywood mentality," he confesses. Going on and on about it is "really frustrating anyway. It's a threat to what you do."

"When I work," he adds, "my agenda is nothing but the movie. Nothing else. When I'm acting, I try to leave a window open for creativity, but I still like to be very open about what I'm thinking about. I try to get so in control that then I get out of control when I act."

Costner now has the necessary experience under his belt after working with such seasoned actors as Connery, De Niro, Hackman and Quinn. As he notes, "I've been around some good actors – Connery, De Niro, Hackman – and they all teach in a man's way, circle the problem, talk about acting generally, don't be too specific, too hurtful, and that in itself is generosity, my friend."

De Palma has said that Costner is "one of those actors who can make all the old cliches seem real again." Oliver Stone is counting on it. *JFK* is an incendiary, political conspiracy thriller that covers one of the most traumatic times in recent American history.

JFK is being produced by Stone and his long-time co-producer A. Kitman Ho (who also worked with Stone on *Platoon, Born On The Fourth Of July, The Doors,* and others). The screenplay is based on Garrison's book *On The Trial Of The Assassins,* Jim Marrs' *Crossfire* and varied public sources of information.

Stone has said we will "learn a lot about the facts which were ignored by the Warren Commission. We're looking at the old evidence and will present alternative scenarios not only based on Jim's account, but from various sources." The director has been developing the picture for over two and a half years and says some liberties will be taken for entertainment purposes. However, he "cannot take many because the material is very important and sacred to the public."

Sacred is the right word. There has been an outcry from many groups and organizations declaring war on Stone and *JFK,* charging that Stone's account is inaccurate and misleading. The film's central belief is that Kennedy was more than likely killed because, had he lived, he would have withdrawn from Vietnam and taken moves set on reducing the tensions of the Cold War. The real powers that be in this country had figured him a threat to national security, the director believes. Stone discovered through Larry Howard, a former Texas contractor who founded the JFK Assassination Information Center in Dallas, a cornucopia of never-before disclosed information. The information includes the following: "the actual rifle that inflicted the fatal head shot, the identity of the person who eliminated key witnesses, the code names of the other gunman involved, a picture of the assassin's wife with Jack Ruby and a letter to the assassin congratulating him on a job well done from a former President of the United States."

Howard reportedly told Stone, "we have uncovered the real truth behind the assassination. JFK was murdered by the real people who control the power base in the U.S. In their minds, he was a threat to national security and had to be eliminated."

The script as written would take more than three hours to film in its entirety, admitted Stone. There are over 1,000 camera set-ups, 95 scenes, 15 different film stocks and endless intercuts and flashbacks. Costner, who was chosen for his "Americanness," is due to receive $7 million plus a percentage of the film's box office gross.

As to the outpouring of criticism directed at the movie, Stone alleges that not all of it is from the critics. "It's still going on and we have to deal with it... There are a lot of obstacles and we've received many warnings from people trying to stop us," he remarks.

There are many current Kennedy-based projects, including the biggest and most successful, Don DeLillo's *Libra*, a work that theorizes Kennedy's assassination was the work of anti-Castro activists. Stone says as far as he is concerned, *Libra* is "fiction, because it has Lee Harvey Oswald pulling the trigger at the Depository, and my film will prove otherwise."

There are rumors that Stone tried to kill similar projects, including A&M Films' option on *Libra*. Stone laughs at this kind of speculation, saying he wishes that kind of power were his. Adds the Oscar-winning and often controversial director, "I'd love to believe that, it gives me a lot of power... Nobody stops projects from being made."

Still, there is more confrontation over this project than Stone has ever faced. At one point, he railed at reporters for their lack of "integrity" and "courage" where their coverage of the Kennedy controversy is concerned: "You should be fucking ashamed of yourself! You call yourself journalists? You're caricatures of journalism! It's not journalism you are doing! It's fucking propaganda. You are working for the Ministry of Information! You have become Winston Smith! You have become George Orwell's creation! You could be a Russian working for Stalin in *Pravda* in 1935! You are liars! You just invent history! You should go back to school and learn honesty!"

Stone is not unknown for these types of outbursts about what displeases him. After all, Warner Brothers had to ignore that fact that before making *JFK* there, he referred to the studio as one of the town's "cocksucking vampires."

Stone initially hoped to interest the studio in a project about the life of Howard Hughes. Terry Semel, impatient with Stone's hostility, finally said, "If you want to make a movie about corruption, the biggest corruption of all is the Kennedy murder." Stone's eyes widened and the Hughes idea was immediately put to rest.

In Stone's script, there are definitely some liberties with the truth, surprising for someone so concerned with people "knowing" their history. For example, Clay Shaw was a refined and dignified man with excellent taste in literature, music and architecture, but in Stone's film, he is painted as a lewd man who grabs young boys (he was a homosexual) in a home that looks "early dungeon" in decor. There have also been charges that, in order to strengthen his conspiracy theory, Stone has "invented characters, transposed scenes and created situations."

Costner and Stone both admit that on evenings they went out during the filming, they frequently "drank too much." The set was not one filled with laughter and Stone was often found complaining. As the man on the hot seat says, "I feel like a presidential candidate, for Christ's sake, going through all this. Why do I have to defend my movie? I'm not running for office and I'm not asking for a reopening of the investigation. I'm making a movie that will come and go."

Costner's next project after *JFK* is already in production. *The Bodyguard* is a picture that promises to be a big box office success, a slick romantic thriller with two major talents, Kevin Costner and Whitney Houston in her screen debut. Houston had searched for the past four years in vain for the right project with which to commence her film career. Arista, her recording studio, has tried for years to develop a project that would adequately showcase the singer's immense talents. They finally found it in the form of Lawrence Kasdan's *The Bodyguard* and Costner as co-star.

Superstar Houston will star with the Academy Award-winning actor as a singer whose life is threatened by a fan when in rides Costner to the rescue as a bodyguard. Costner describes Houston as loaded with cinematic potential and says he wanted her for the role.

As the hit singer recalls, "Kevin said to me, 'I know you can do it; I know you can act. I want you.' He was very excited when he saw the screen test." The film is currently shooting and will be released in the summer of 1992.

The story does not sound like it will keep Houston's sunny image alive with fans, who will no doubt be disappointed to find out that being a top recording star is no fun because you have to fear for your life. The film's box office potential is also risky at best as it is not in keeping with the message in Houston's music that she is carefree, has fun and basically focuses on the love in the world, not the violence. Besides that, critics may now attack Costner due to his growing ego and power in a town that begrudges both. He has already begun to get less-than-glowing press releases.

As reported by *The Hollywood Reporter's* Martin Grove, Costner "has become the *bete noire* for the media." Backing this opinion was a piece by Maureen Dowd of *The New York Times*: "Kevin Costner is in a bad mood. It has been said that Mr. Costner is worried about his thinning hair. His hair looks O.K. It's his thinning skin he should be worried about." Pauline Kael replied, "Costner has feathers in his hair and feathers in his head."

Yet there are just as many industry insiders whose conception of Costner is at the opposite end of the spectrum. As reported by Nancy Griffin of *Premiere* Magazine, "Kevin's the real thing."

Some, including critic Kenneth Turan of *The Los Angeles Times*, feels Costner is getting too big for his proverbial britches: "Like many actors, he's very successful in certain roles. His best parts have been where he is a seeker of something, where he's dissatisfied with the world and looks for something better. I don't think he's good as a leader of men." It's true that the self-pleasing and reticent nature of Costner's characters makes them much more selfish than a real leader of men can be but *No Way Out* Producer Mace Neufeld defends the star by saying that "I don't think Costner's going down a typical path and there are bumps along every road. Part of his intelligence as an actor is his ability to analyze stories. He's a sensible fellow and very talented. He's in the tradition of the old stars like John Wayne and Gary Cooper. He's the kind of guy that you'd like to have as a friend. He'll be around a long time."

The Bodyguard is written and produced by co-partners Costner, Jim Wilson, and long-time Costner associate, Lawrence Kasdan. The screenplay is Kasdan's and Mick Jackson directs the picture. Costner's character, an ex-Secret Service agent hired to protect Houston's character, a high-profile actress-singer who is threatened by an obsessed fan. The film promises to be a slick action thriller. Whether Houston will perform songs in the film has as yet not been determined.

The future is an unknown for all of us, but Costner says one thing is certain, he will continue to develop his own material. "The thing is, movies crop up. There's the winter movies, the spring movies, the fall movies. I'm not always impressed with the movies that happen to be coming out. And if they're not there, then you either have to jump into one – and I know what it's like to be on a movie for four months that's not going right – or sit it out – and I know what it's like to sit it out. And so the only option – and you don't have to be a genius to figure it out – is to just begin to develop materials that reflect your sensibility. And be able, then, to slot them in."

In spite of all the controversy surrounding the movie about the late President, Costner is finding time these days to be chummy with some politicians of his own. Long known for his conservative and Republican sympathies where politics is concerned, Costner has been photographed with Republican Senator Phil Gramm of Texas, whom he reportedly has advanced $4,000 for his 1996 bid for the Presidential race.

However, Gramm is not the only politician friend Costner can count on these days. In July of 1991, Costner and Andre Agassi joined none other than President George Bush at Camp David. The Commander-In-Chief was there to prepare for his weekend summit with Mikhail Gorbachev but managed to get in 18 holes of golf with Agassi and Costner, who "got creamed," as Costner confessed. Bush agreed, saying, "I hope that the summit goes better than the golf with these guys."

As to the future, Costner is unsure of what it may hold and a little afraid success may begin to take its toll. However, he is sure he is happy with his past. As he states, "I'm pleased with the choices I've made. I try to take a lot of time deciding what movie I'll do. That's why you don't see me going from movie to movie. I believe in the movie experience. I think that if people choose to follow your name, you've got to be semi-honorable to that, and try to put value up there when they see that name."

It's good to see Costner's satisfaction with his past choices, but it is quite a questionable matter to state one's goal is to be "semi-" honorable.

Costner has also admitted that the future may hold

more than movies for him. "I'd like to get a handle on who I am. I know I'm changing. Maybe I've got to go someplace else. I'm not searching for a way out, but I keep thinking I'd like to coach a Little League team for Joe or something, you know." Since Joe is only two, we can safely assume it will be some time in the future.

The future holds much promise for the self-described "skinny rat" from Compton. In addition to Orion's *Mick* and *American Hero* and Warner Brothers' *The Bodyguard*, he will more than likely develop projects through his association with Warner Brothers. He also keeps bringing up the subject of doing a remake of *Camelot* because of his feelings about King Arthur. Perhaps this is because "Camelot" describes all that is good to this would-be "good guy."

Or maybe it reminds him of the innocent and hopeful America at the time of John Kennedy's reign as President. Possibly, he is just in the "Camelot" frame since he has just completed a film about the assassination of the President whose time was known for its Camelot-like magic.

For a final word from the man who would be boy, here are his feelings about a potential future project that seems to bring out the "tingle" in him he remembers experiencing from the films he watched as a child:

"The one role I'd really love to play is King Arthur. No kidding. I can sing good [has he read the Hillburn review?]. I started singing in choir at school, in musicals. That's how I started acting. Richard Harris I loved; he sings with great commitment, and I don't imagine that Arthur was that great a singer. I just imagine him as being a really good man who is faced with incredible dilemmas."

"The story always gets me. This guy Lancelot comes in and you're saying, 'Go the fuck away' and he stays. When

Mordrid enters you say, 'Kill that fucker, kill that little son of a bitch before he fucks up everything.' Nobody does. And then there's Guinevere: 'Stop fucking around. Quit fucking Arthur around. You made a mistake! Go back to Arthur.' And she doesn't. She goes to a nunnery instead."

From his description, it seems the story of Camelot retains the requisite filmmaking passion that is necessary for a Kevin Costner project.